Dr Angela Shier-Jones is a presbyte
and is a member of the Connexion
is mandated to support and encoura¡
throughout the British Methodist Churᵤₕ. ₋
lications include the edited volume *The Making of Ministry* ₐₙ₋
(with Luke Curran) *Methodist Present Potential.*

SPCK Library of Ministry

Community and Ministry: An introduction to community
development in a Christian context
Paul Ballard and Lesley Husselbee

Pioneer Ministry and Fresh Expressions of Church
Angela Shier-Jones

Reader Ministry Explored
Cathy Rowling and Paula Gooder

Skills for Collaborative Ministry
Sally Nash, Jo Pimlott and Paul Nash

Supporting New Ministers in the Local Church: A handbook
Keith Lamdin and David Tilley

Tools for Reflective Ministry
Sally Nash and Paul Nash

PIONEER MINISTRY
AND
FRESH EXPRESSIONS
OF CHURCH

SPCK Library of Ministry

ANGELA SHIER-JONES

First published in Great Britain in 2009

Society for Promoting Christian Knowledge
36 Causton Street
London SW1P 4ST

British Library Cataloguing-in-Publication Data
A catalogue record for this book is available from the British Library

ISBN 978–0–281–06113–6

1 3 5 7 9 10 8 6 4 2

Typeset by Graphicraft Limited, Hong Kong
Printed in Great Britain by MPG

Produced on paper from sustainable forests

This book is dedicated to the past and present pioneers of the Church. It is offered in humble thanks to those shapers and makers of Christian communities who, having sought and found the lost, continued to search until they also found a way of enthusing and motivating them to become disciples of the living Word

In particular it is dedicated to past and present ministerial students of the South East Institute of Theological Education and of Wesley College Bristol. Their passion for God and their commitment to the people of God have taught me and inspired me and given me great hope for the future of the Church

Contents

Contents

Part 2
CONGREGATIONS AND PIONEER MINISTRY

Introduction

> We continually may need to ask ourselves whether the church needs
> to be reinvented or whether it is simply a matter of rediscovering
> the church's original purpose, mission, and ministry. Or more likely,
> is it a matter of creatively blending rediscovery and reengineering
> so the church can meet the urgent personal and social concerns
> of the 21st century?[1]

Sociologists have proved that all human organizations, move-
ments and institutions have a life-cycle whose stages can effectively be predicted as it moves from origination to closure, from
birth to death. Inasmuch as a local church or focused community
behaves like a human institution, it too can be seen to undergo
the same cyclic structure. It all begins in a dream. The dream
fosters belief which invites certain goals to be set. The goals
necessitate frameworks or structures to be built to support and
substantiate the growth that belief in the goals has created. At its
peak, the community becomes missional – fulfilling the goals and
objectives of the original dream. But then, for a variety of reasons,
the dream begins to fade. Nostalgia sets in as people remember
what the dream once was rather than allow themselves to be motivated by it. After nostalgia comes the questioning, when people
wonder what has been lost, what has gone wrong, why growth
is no longer happening. These questions become ever more
critical until the few who remain are often polarized, divided
and uncertain as to the right direction to take. It is this which
ultimately, inevitably leads to the collapse of the community or
the closure of the church. The dream has ended.

Experience teaches us that it is generally at the nostalgia or
questioning stage that church people begin to search for new
ways to mission and for easy solutions to the problem. Often the
proposed solution does nothing more than speed up the demise
because it replaces or is in direct conflict with the originating
dream. Tim Keel, the minister of a fresh expression of church in
the USA called Jacob's Well, has criticized the recurrent search for

techniques of church growth, well aware that churches that have followed other trends, whether the Alpha[2] course or Purpose-Driven Life studies, are likely to try out aspects of the emergent church movement from which his ministry comes. He refutes (as he wrote in an essay in *The Relevant Church*) the idea that 'if only we can (re)discover x (fill-in-the-blank: prayer, fasting, worship, community, drama, service) and implement it, then the Church will have y (fill-in-the-blank: impact, relevance, meaning, validity, profile, etc.)'.[3] His criticism is well founded. Not only do such searches for a 'solution' make the mistake of prioritizing the Church over and above the community's relationship with God, but they also presuppose that human techniques can usurp or even supplant God's work of grace.

The very idea that mission can be pre-programmed, packaged and purchased makes a mockery of the concept of the Church as the body of Christ, a dynamic mutually indwelling community of grace, unless of course, it is believed that the essence of Christ is so easily condensed and marketed! This does not mean that the Church should not consider 'proven' strategies or programmes for mission and ministry; there is, after all, no point in reinventing the wheel. Deliberate theological and practical reflection will, however, prove far more fruitful and beneficial than 'off-the-shelf solutions'.

Searches for 'successful forms' of fresh expressions or pioneer ministry that can be copied elsewhere may be well-intentioned but are usually misguided. The search is premised on the idea that people are basically the same everywhere, and that what works for one will usually work for all. The importance of contextualization is often lost in the race to run a 'successful' Alpha course, café church, messy church, pub-prophets, disciple course, Emmaus course, cycle-Christians, book-believers, parent club, skateboard church, internet church, community church, pioneer ministry, etc. Love of neighbour can be lost in the love of success that such programmes seem to promise. Contextualization is often only paid lip-service to by offering tea and shepherd's pie on the local Alpha course rather than wine and a three-course meal.

This book contains many examples of pioneer ministries and fresh expressions of church that have emerged out of the response of a team or an individual to a vision given to them by God for a particular community. They are offered as illustrations, and examples of how the pioneering spirit can be released, not as guaranteed programmes that will ensure 'success' if they are cloned. None of what is contained in this book can replace a vision from God. All that a book such as this can ever realistically provide is assistance in how to identify the vision and release the potential that God has given to each unique context, and help in avoiding common mistakes. By providing examples of good practice, and of what has worked elsewhere, along with the theological background and foundational teaching that underpins it, it is hoped that those who are willing to pioneer a new ministry might be inspired and encouraged to work towards making the dream that God has given them a reality.

Unless the LORD builds the house, those who build it labour in vain.
(Ps. 127.1)

There are two distinct parts to this book. Part 1, the first four chapters, is written primarily for pioneers and explores how to begin and develop a pioneer ministry and initiate fresh expressions of church. It does not presume that the pioneer minister is either ordained or belongs to a particular denomination, although the chapters do address some of the key questions being asked by members of the main Protestant traditions. It is hoped that the pioneer who reads this will want to work with the inherited Church. The advice contained in this section however applies equally well to those who are compelled to leave the systems and structures of the inherited Church to follow wherever the wind of the Spirit might lead them. The history of the Church teaches that there have always been prophets and evangelists who work from outside of the institutional Church to fashion the future freedoms to follow Christ, just as there have always been those who work within the Church to fashion the future disciplines of discipleship. To those who are called to leave, we simply ask that if they do so because they are following Christ, they leave clear markers for the rest of the Church to follow if and when it is called to do so.

The second part of the book, Chapters 5 through to 8, is written for congregations who are interested in working with pioneer ministers. In particular, it is written to assist congregations and pioneer ministers who are currently serving in a local church setting, to plan a future mission strategy together. It provides practical guidelines and assistance for becoming a pioneering church rather than an inherited church which has a pioneer minister. Existing churches have very real assets that can be used to release the pioneering potential of the Church, the most obvious being its buildings, and its people. Part 2 presumes a willingness on the part of the church to commit time and energy into being part of a tremendously exciting adventure in the history of the Church, for the sake of the gospel, rather than for the sake of increasing church attendance.

Parts 1 and 2 are both written from a distinctively and unashamedly theological perspective. This is not yet another book on how to make churches grow or how to start a fresh expression. You will look in vain for the marketing and advertising slogans or branded and promotional success stories. This is a book about God and ministry. In particular it is about the calling of God to some people to minister to the unchurched people of God such that the gospel can be heard by them. It is above all a book that urges and encourages those who have heard Christ say 'Follow me' to follow him out of the doors of the church and into the world that God loves.

Part 1

HOW TO BEGIN AND DEVELOP A PIONEER MINISTRY

1

Defining

Who or what is a pioneer minister?

Someone wading through the wealth of material available on the internet on pioneer ministers and fresh expressions of church in the Church of England or the Methodist Church could be forgiven for assuming that all pioneer ministers are young, energetic, IT savvy, wear jeans and polo shirts, and are predominantly (although not exclusively) middle-class. In reality however pioneer ministers are called into ministry at varying ages, out of all races and social classes, and include people of every gender, culture and context, with a range of different physical and mental attributes.

> We're looking for people who combine Christian maturity with a concern for those outside the Christian community; ministers who are willing to learn as they go, try new things and have the vision and skills to develop new communities who do some things differently.[1]

The term 'pioneer minister' is not meant to conjure up the image of a particular sort of person but of a particular sort of ministerial conduct or focus set within the much wider framework of the Church.

As it is used in this book, the term 'pioneer minister' developed out of reflection in the Church of England on the language and terminology of the report *Mission-Shaped Church*. The expression 'pioneer church planters' used in that report was dismissed because it seemed too restrictive and failed to take into account the diversity of fresh expressions of church. The expression 'pioneer missional leaders' seemed to capture more of the missional intent of the document but it ran the risk of creating too simplistic an association between ordained ministry and leadership in mission. Leading mission is only a part of the calling of the ordained. As the *Bishops' Guidelines* stated, 'All ministers are called to be "missional", not only those who are called to pioneer ministry.'[2] The term 'pioneer minister' was eventually chosen so as to make it perfectly clear that pioneer ministry is not part of a different *category* or class of lay or ordained ministry but a distinctive *focus* of ministry. This is what enables the term to be understood outside of the Anglican Communion, and recognized as something held in common with circuit ministers, mission pastors and emergent church leaders. All of these are called to a ministry in which pioneering initiatives such as fresh expressions of church are intended to be the primary focus.

A brief aside is perhaps needed about the differences between parochial, local and circuit ministry, which led to the recognition of ordained pioneering ministry within the Church of England. The recent publication by the Fresh Expressions team has suggested that it could be helpful to divide ordained ministry into three dimensions or areas of work as quoted below:

- Sustaining existing communities in mission through the ministries of Word and Sacrament (which we call priestly or presbyteral ministry).
- Leadership and oversight of other ministries and a network of communities and churches (which we call the exercise of episcope – literally watching over).
- Working to serve the wider community as a bearer of good news and pioneering new communities of faith (which we call the ministry of evangelism or diaconal ministry).[3]

These divisions may be helpful in an Anglican or Roman Catholic context as both denominations have a threefold cumulative understanding of ministry. In a Methodist, United Reformed Church, Baptist or other Free Church context, however, such divisions can be very misleading, appearing to create a distinction where none currently exists between the work of a pioneer minister and that of a local church minister/presbyter or priest. In the case of Methodism, which has two distinct non-cumulative orders of ministry, it could also give the impression that only deacons are called to pioneer ministry, something which many within the Church would want to challenge. The dilemma is exacerbated by the influence that the Anglican parish system has had on the expectations of congregations of all mainstream churches following the steady erosion of traditional denominational allegiances. The model of the traditional parish priest, ministering to a single geographically bounded community of people who regularly attend 'church', has unfortunately become superimposed on the significantly different role of Methodist and other Free Church ministers. The proportion of ministerial time committed to pioneering as opposed to pastoring in the nonconformist and Free Church traditions has, as might be expected, tended to be significantly higher than in the established churches.

Wesley for example included the following warning for those tempted to model their ministry on parish ministry:

> Observe: It is not your business to preach so many times, and to take care merely of this or that Society, but to save as many souls as you can; to bring as many sinners as you possibly can to repentance; and, with all your power, to build them up in that holiness, without which they cannot see the Lord.[4]

Ordained pioneer ministers are a separate category of ministry in the Anglican Church primarily because of the way in which the Anglican Church trains and deploys its priests. They tend not to be a separate category in most Free Churches because the existing definition of ministry tends to be less bounded or geographically constrained in those Churches.

> I have not thought of myself as a Pioneer, just as a Methodist Minister. The extent to which I am a 'pioneer' comes from just getting on with normal ministry but attempting to do so at modern society speeds rather than 18th century church speeds.[5]

Can an Anglican parish priest have a pioneering ministry without being formally recognized as a pioneer minister? Of course, particularly when the local congregation and parish register include a significant number of 'unchurched' people – as most do. The creation of a specific category of ordained ministry in the Church of England is not meant to constrict or stifle existing pioneering ministry. On the contrary, it is hoped that it will actively encourage and enable people who might not otherwise recognize they have a calling to ordained ministry.

The creation and implementation of the Ordained Pioneer Ministry scheme of the Church of England has unfortunately encouraged the mistaken belief that pioneer ministry is primarily the preserve of the clergy. Nothing could be further from the truth. Across the denominations, if historical evidence can be used as any guide, only a small percentage of pioneer ministers will ever be ordained. For every apostle in the early Church there were always a significantly larger number engaged in mission and outreach. They pioneered the growth of the Church alongside the apostles and explored new ways in which people that they lived and worked among could participate in the life of the body of Christ. There is no reason to suppose that this particular phase of kingdom growth will be any different from those of previous generations.

Whether exercised by a member of the laity, a deacon, bishop, priest, pastor, or minister, pioneer ministry is a vocation. It is a calling to something which is so intrinsically related to the personal gifts and abilities of a person that it is best undertaken only by those uniquely suited to it. In this it is no different from all Christian vocations. Every person is uniquely equipped by God for the role that they are called to perform within the kingdom for the life of the body of Christ. In the case of pioneer ministers, more is currently known of the nature of the work to be done than of the full range of gifts and graces necessary to do it. God is calling and equipping pioneer ministers to share in the imaginative, creative, ongoing tasks of reconciliation and celebration that will enable others to be in communion with Christ to the glory of God the Father in the power of the Holy Spirit. They are called to do this in ways that are fresh, authentic, culturally and contextually sensitive and which will not harm in any way what God has already done, and is doing in the lives of others.

The Church is expressed in fresh ways in each generation in response to new questions and new challenges. These different understandings or experiences often question attitudes that were once taken for granted. Fresh expressions of church has been defined as a form of church for our changing culture established primarily for the benefit of people who are not yet members of any church. It will come into being through principles of listening, service, incarnational mission and making disciples. It will have the potential to become a mature expression of church shaped by the gospel and the enduring marks of the church for its cultural context.[6]

Not every fresh expression of church will be initiated by a pioneer minister or form part of a pioneering ministry. The difference lies in the fact that pioneering ministry is not about trying to persuade people to belong to the Church; it is about belonging and ministering to God's people in the world in such a way that every community is transformed into church. Not church in the sense of a building with a gathered community and a weekly God-slot with its predictable diet of liturgy and worship, teaching, fellowship and, of course, the offertory. But church in the sense of a Christian community aware of the presence of God, seeking to follow the way of Christ and open to the transforming power of the Holy Spirit wherever it happens to be in the world. Members of such churches are usually called to live and exist within the secular world, rather than separate from it. They seldom retreat to places of sanctuary once a week. Instead they find or form sanctuary in the everyday spaces and places in their life, in the workplace, the home, the gymnasium, bingo hall, and so on. The pioneer's calling is to help people to do just that. They share the gospel with them in such a way that it adds to whatever is already of God in their lives and inspires and enables them to grow as disciples of Christ.

> The shape of the church is a response to a societal attitude, and the church cannot be understood historically save as an institution in dialogue with its world.[7]

This secular postmodern, post-atheist world is not devoid of God. God cannot be expelled from creation nor kept from the people. The Church has inadvertently separated itself from its primary calling, to share in the reconciliation of all God's people and the transformation of society, by creating a sharp distinction between the secular and the holy. A significant number of churches are shut from Monday through to Saturday, when people are expected to live their everyday lives. Only on Sunday, and usually only for an hour, are the populace invited in to the holy place called God's house. Pioneer ministry ends that separation by working to highlight the holy in the secular. It attempts to show how, in Christ, the secular world can grow to a new maturity by moving beyond where it is at present in terms of its over-fixation on modernity, affluence and sophistication. Through pioneer ministry, God is calling the secular world to be transformed not by returning to a former conservatism or subservience to an institutional Church, but by growing into something new, 'a post-modernity, a post-affluence, and a post-sophistication which celebrates the simplicity and honesty of the power of God's loving presence in the world'.[8]

Fresh expressions of church

Most fresh expressions of church arise naturally out of a local church's participation in the *Missio Dei*, or mission of God. Whenever ministers or members of congregations design and provide alternative, culturally sensitive, worship for the unchurched people in their locality, they are creating a fresh expression of church. Youth fellowships, student missions, even parent and toddler groups, can all justifiably be called fresh expressions of church if, that is, they are held and conducted as a form of church and as a service to the community. There is, however, more to a fresh expression of church than experiments in sound, lighting, space, or even ways of being community. A kibbutz or a commune is not a church, even though its members have chosen to live and work together in peace for the common good.

Fresh expressions of church should still be church. No matter how alternative their worship is or how specific or tightly focused they are as a community, they should still be characteristically and recognizably 'one, holy, catholic and apostolic' in nature. The Gathering Place in South Wales, for example, has now been operating for over a year next to an estate where there has been little provision made for the local community. In addition to providing space for various activities throughout the week such as parent and toddler groups, coffee mornings, etc., the Gathering Place hosts a fresh expression of church on Sundays called Mosaic. What started as a once a month gathering place for the unchurched has now matured into a weekly café style service attended by up to 25 people keen to explore relevant issues and look at what Christianity has to say. It could of course be argued that to expect pioneering initiatives to conform to traditional or historical distillations of what it means to be church is to miss the point of what Fresh Expressions is all about. The invitation to live and work within the faith and unity of the one, holy, catholic and apostolic Church should not be understood in any restrictive or prescriptive way but in a way that is liberating, even surprising.[9] If an initiative is an expression of church, rather than an expression of the egos or personalities of the initiating ministers or congregations, then it will exhibit the characteristic marks of a Christian community.

The Church is one

Fresh expressions of church formed in response to a pioneering ministry, in spite of how they are often perceived, are not a threat to the unity of the Church. It is in its unity in Christ that all ministry finds its fullest expression. The Church is the body of Christ, and its unity is not something that ministers, pioneering or otherwise, can either create or destroy. Pioneer ministers are seldom called to create community, still less to separate out specific communities from the body of Christ. On the contrary they are most often called to minister to the members of existing communities. As a result of the fragmentation of society and its proliferation of alternative community values, people are often unaware of their place within the overall unity of the people of God and the body of Christ. The Church of the Good Shepherd in the Methodist Circuit of Shrewsbury was set up to try and counter at least one aspect of this fragmentation of society – the alienation of the elderly. This particular fresh expression of church was deliberately targeted to reach out to older people and to the housebound and address their pastoral and spiritual needs. In addition to offering prayer, comfort and spiritual support, this particular fresh expression of church also provides the opportunity for its members to receive 'Extended Holy Communion',[10] and in so doing, it affirms the conviction that God's people are one – 'Though we are many, we are one body, because we all share in one bread.'[11]

Pioneer ministries try to address the sin of separation and independence and participate in the reconciling ministry of Christ. By the grace of God and in the power of the Holy Spirit, they can enable individuals or whole communities to be reconciled to their belonging in Christ, and so be incorporated into the unity that is Christ. As Trish Clavert of the Church of the Good Shepherd states: 'I am always looking for ways we can include the housebound in the life of the local church.'[12] Through newsletters and common resources she encourages the sense of unity and belonging that is characteristic of church. This does not mean that fresh expressions of church will ultimately merge or unite with traditional forms of church as that would presume that traditional church is the desired 'norm' or 'right form' of church. Denominationalism makes it all too evident that what we consider to be traditional forms of church are no more 'real', 'true', or 'normal' forms of church than fresh expressions of church are.

Holy

In spite of the fact that they are often called out of traditional or mainstream churches to practise their ministry, pioneer ministers are not more holy, gifted or 'religious' than any other Christian. The communities that they gather together or assist in transforming may feel more 'holy' when, for example, the worship which is offered deliberately stimulates the spiritual senses, but this should not be mistaken for the holiness that is a characteristic of the Church. A fresh expression of church initiated by a pioneer minister will be recognizably holy, not because of its worship, or even because of the piety of the pioneer, but because its members attempt to reflect the love of Christ in their love and care for each other. Any expression of church is holy if and when, as a community, it exists solely to follow the Holy One, Jesus, and in so doing attempts to be a temple for the Holy Spirit. It is holy when it becomes a means whereby the truth and nature of God can be expressed and people are enabled to grow in grace and holiness. 'Glorious', for example, is a sacramental fresh expression of church that combines community transformation, radical worship and youth ministry in the Diocese of Southwark, South London. It is not a regular and self-sustaining community, but rather an occasional gathering to inspire people. When it does meet, Glorious uses the creative arts to try and transcend the divides in the community of Peckham, a place currently struggling with knife crime and youth gangs. As Toby Wright notes, this fresh expression has much in common with the vision of the Anglo-Catholic tradition in the nineteenth century in its desire to engage with people and seek social and spiritual transformation.[13]

It is not the act of being separated out of society or a particular cultural or even religious context that makes a fresh expression of church holy. Members are seldom removed from their context, and the pioneering ministry that they receive does not shield them or offer them an escape from the necessity of dealing with the pressures of life. On the contrary, each reconciled community, as with every other expression of church, has to work out its own salvation by striving after and living in the hope of holiness. As with every part of Christ's Church, fresh expressions of church are called to be holy in the tension between their actual, separated and fallible historical existence, and their essential being as part of the body of Christ, God's holy people.

Catholic

Pioneer ministry often begins with a prophetic longing for and vision of the reconciliation of a particular section of society or group within it: the skateboarding youngsters on a built-up housing estate, the online community, single parents, stockbrokers, street walkers, dog walkers, artists, shop assistants, commuters . . . the list is as endless as the human capacity to separate and compartmentalize itself. In spite of seeming to have a very narrow focus, any fresh expression of church initiated by a minister by the grace of God will be an expression of the catholicity of the body of Christ. This is because every fresh expression is a deliberate attempt to provide a means of including into the body of Christ whole communities that might otherwise have been excluded. A good example of what is meant is found in John's

Gospel, where it is made clear that Jesus came first to minister to the Jewish people. Nonetheless, the Gospel narrates how, as a result of a single specific moment of his ministry to a woman at a well and to the people of her village in Samaria, Jesus extended the body of believers to include those who would normally have been excluded by virtue of their ethnicity: Jews have nothing to do with Samaritans. Even though Samaritans could not become Jews, as a consequence of Jesus' ministry to them they were able to know the Messiah, and to believe that God's plan of salvation was for them as well as for the Jews. The pioneer minister helps to express the catholicity of the body of Christ by modelling in his or her ministry the fact that in spite of humanity's best efforts to segregate and exclude, God will find a way of integrating and including all of humanity into the body of Christ. There is no culture or context that God cannot call someone to speak the truth into. Revive, for example, is a mature fresh expression of church in Leeds, which is more than a decade old. Its founder Simon Hall says that 'Revive is mainly made up of people who didn't fit into "regular" Church. They were too cynical, too rebellious, too radical, too charismatic.'[14] Its particular focus on the so-called 'missing generation' (those aged between 20 and 40) does not intentionally exclude others, but it does enable those who might otherwise feel excluded from church to experience the all-inclusive nature of God's love.

Apostolic

Lastly, a fresh expression of church resulting from the ministry of a pioneer will be apostolic by virtue of its adherence to the apostolic teachings of the Church and by the way in which it is missional. A pioneering fresh expression of church is usually apostolic inasmuch as it shares with the original apostles a willingness to be sent into the world to participate in God's creative and reconciling purposes. The two strands of being apostolic, namely being related to the apostolic Church and participating in the *Missio Dei*, cannot be separated without losing something intrinsic to what it means to be apostolic.

The term apostolic has connotations of structure and order as well as mission and evangelism. Scripture records that not all were called to be apostles, and the early Church clearly differentiated between the different vocations that they felt the Spirit had enabled them to identify. Something known or assumed about the nature or authority of what it was to be an apostle, for an example, undoubtedly lay behind Paul's vehement insistence on his own apostolic credentials before the church at Galatia. The belief is that being an apostolic church also implies (albeit indirectly) being an authoritative or structured church. Of all the characteristics of church this is the one which is most discriminating:

> of all the charges laid at the door of the church by many disaffected young people . . . the most frequent and damning is the charge of controlling leadership . . . stifling creativity, stunting innovation and imagination, forcing uniformity, silencing dissent.[15]

Nonetheless, every valid fresh expression of church or pioneer ministry will be related to the Church not only by its adherence to the apostolic creeds and doctrines, but also by its submission to the authority of the Church as it expresses it in terms of both oversight and order. This does not mean that all fresh expressions of church or pioneering ministries have to conform to one particular denomination's authority or hierarchical structures, but it cannot be independent of the Church. To be recognized as church, a fresh expression must accept and embrace the authority, order and oversight of Christ and those whom Christ has called and appointed as apostles. This may vary from denomination to denomination, but it always exists. While there are many who would argue that the time has come for a totally unstructured form of church leadership, the Scriptures seem to suggest that this is neither ideal nor realistic. God's repeated action in creation is to bring order out of chaos; a chaotic church is an oxymoron. Thus, the acceptance of the necessity of authority, oversight and order, while uncomfortable to many fresh expressions of church, is nonetheless an intrinsic part of what it means to be authentically church.

As so many contributors to *The Call and the Commission*[16] have pointed out, the way in which leadership is exercised today is very different from that of twenty years ago. Programmes such as *The Apprentice* demonstrate the stress that is placed on character, initiative, drive, ingenuity and risk-taking skills. Knowledge and specialisms are things that can be 'bought in'. Charisma and imagination, determination and commitment matter more. Unsurprisingly therefore, many forms of fresh expression have evolved a different form of apostolic leadership, one that is less clerically dependent (the priest's knowledge and sacramental specialisms can be 'bought in' if required). The 'priesthood of all believers' does not mean democratic church leadership, but freedom from clerically dominated leadership. One example of how this has worked in practice is found in 'Mind the Gap', a fresh expression of church formed in 2001 in the Gateshead and Jarrow Methodist Circuit. As part of its growing maturity, Mind the Gap was able to fulfil one of its original visions for its ministry in 2008 by making the transition from ordained to indigenous lay leadership with the full support of the circuit leadership team.

There are of course other ways in which fresh expressions of church can be authenticated. Many new forms of church prefer to describe themselves as communities that are modelled on Trinitarian or perichoretic principles. This, as Ian Mobsby points out,[17] resonates strongly with postmodern forms of ecclesiology like that of Grenz, who writes:

> In the end, participation in the perichoretic dance of the triune God as those who by the Spirit are in Christ is what constitutes community in the highest sense and hence marks the true church . . .[18]

These methods of authentication do not invalidate the creedal marks of the Church. They simply offer an alternative means of expressing them. At a time when the very word church is often thought of as part of the problem rather than the solution to increasing secularization and alienation, alternative means of authenticating embryonic forms of Christian community can be very helpful.

The pioneer minister's task is not to try and fill the void caused by the absence of spirituality in community by any and every means possible, but to initiate fresh ways of being church. Regardless of whether it refers to itself as 'church' or as a Christian community, those who are outside of it will still tend to see it as representative of the object of its worship – of God. It is this that makes it essential, even if it is uncomfortable, to have a means of evaluating the authenticity of a fresh expression as church or Christian community. The amazingly creative and imaginative opportunities provided by the internet, modern communication technologies, networking and the media invite correspondingly amazing opportunities to misrepresent the gospel and the nature of God. Care is needed.

Having explored the marks of a church as they relate to pioneering initiatives, it is now possible to begin to recognize the charisms and skills needed by pioneer ministers if they are to succeed in pioneering and initiating them.

Pioneering skills

Ministerial gifts are not reserved for the ordained. All Christians share in the ministry of Christ by virtue of their participation in the body of Christ, and as is already evident throughout the emergent church movement and the fresh expressions of church initiative, God is clearly calling both lay and ordained pioneer ministers. On the whole, the skills normally associated with pioneer ministry are not those traditionally thought of as pertaining directly or solely to ordained ministry.

> Pioneers don't always fit neatly into other people's systems. They are more comfortable at the margins. They may not always turn up to the right meetings or fill in the forms. They almost certainly will not volunteer for the 'normal' kind of jobs in church life.[19]

The Church of England's guidelines for the identification, training and deployment of ordained pioneer ministers contains the recommendation that:

> Bishops' Advisers should watch for candidates who have the necessary vision and gifts to be missionary entrepreneurs: to lead fresh expressions of church and forms of church appropriate to a particular culture . . .

It goes on to suggest that the Bishops' Advisers should be on the look-out for 'particular experience and a strong track record in pioneering ministries'. Although there is no intention to form a standardized category of Lay Pioneer Minister within the Church of England, the Church nonetheless recognizes that similar skills to those expected of ordained pioneer ministers will be needed. In particular:

- a vision for planting fresh expressions of church within contemporary culture;
- a developing understanding of the interaction between gospel and culture;
- a mature and developed faith and devotional life;
- the ability and desire to work collaboratively;
- gifts in enabling evangelism and concern for those outside the churches;
- the ability to nurture and grow Christian community;
- the maturity to represent the Christian community appropriately to those outside the churches;
- the capacity to be a bridge and connection between existing forms of church and fresh expressions of church.[20]

The Methodist Church similarly expects to be able to find some evidence of a calling to pioneer ministry before being willing to include the minister (lay or ordained) on an approved list of 'pioneers'. To quote from a recent report:

> The selection process will seek to identify patterns of behaviour (not necessarily in the specific area of beginning Fresh expressions) which are focused around entrepreneurial skills. They will include: vision, motivation, the ability to inspire others, understanding of unchurched culture, healthy work/life balance, natural relationship builder, commitment to holistic church growth, responsive to community, utilizing the gifts of others, flexibility, team builder, resilient, exercising faith (within the discipline of a 'rule of life'?).[21]

Both the Bishops' Guidelines and the Methodist report seem to suggest that the Church has a rather functional view of ministry, which governs its discernment processes. They both seem to imply that the only way in which the Church will recognize and train people to be able to lead or initiate a pioneer ministry is if they are already engaged in some form of pioneering ministry. The truth of the matter however is more complex.

Scripturally, there is very little support for the idea that a calling to any sort of ministry, pioneering or otherwise, can or should be discerned solely by an evaluation of existing skills. The most competent leaders and innovators do not always make the best pioneer ministers. Paul and Jeremiah, two great pioneers, one apostolic, the other prophetic, were only too aware of how inadequately prepared they were for the tasks that God had called them to. Paul wrote his letters painfully aware that it was being said of him: 'His letters are weighty and strong, but his bodily presence is weak, and his speech contemptible' (2 Cor. 10.10). Jeremiah, like many pioneer ministers, had doubts about his age (Jer. 1.5).

Even if there remains an assumption within the Church that pioneer ministry is best done by those with the necessary entrepreneurial or leadership skills, there is generally a conviction within the pioneers themselves that ministry entails something more. John Wesley would have agreed. The essential qualities necessary are those derived not from human skill but from God's grace. Ministry requires grace and charism. Wesley insisted:

> For what are all other gifts, whether natural or acquired, when compared to the grace of God? And how ought this to animate and govern the whole intention, affection, and practice of a minister of Christ.[22]

Thankfully, Scripture narrates the confidence as well as the doubt of those who were pioneers for God's kingdom. When really faced with the challenge of doing God's will, Paul, Jeremiah, Gideon, Moses, Amos, Barnabas, along with the disciples, were convinced that God's Spirit would somehow equip them with whatever gifts and graces were necessary for their calling – even if that took the form of the assistance of another person as in the case of Aaron with Moses. Their relationship with God and the people of God engendered in them a deep trust that God could always overcome, or even use, whatever shortcoming they might have (whether real or imagined). From Moses' inability to speak, Gideon's lack of confidence, Peter's lack of trust, through to Paul's thorn in the flesh. If their ministry was of God, then God would find a way to bless it. The fruit of ministry is always dependent on the gifts and graces, that is the charisms, that flow from God, not the skill or eloquence borne of human endeavours.

Although pioneer ministry is ultimately dependent on the gifts of grace, this does not excuse the pioneer for bad practices which could be put right with appropriate training. Listening skills, for example, can be taught in such a way that they enhance the gift of discernment, enabling pioneers to relate even better to the persons they seek to minister to. Similarly, lessons in public speaking or the good use of rhetoric can assist pioneers to speak the truth so that it can be heard. As Croft notes:

> The idea that a person called to pioneer ministry (or any other ministry) has all the gifts they need and has nothing more to learn seems extremely dangerous. One of the essential elements of this kind of ministry is being open to learn new things in and from every situation.[23]

All pioneer ministers should expect to undertake training in Christian formation, ecclesiology, missiology, reflective practice, and formal theology as well as 'specialist training in inculturation and cross cultural mission'.[24] Such training enables pioneers to understand and think in the terms of the culture in which they are pioneering and to be able to make the connections between that culture and inherited church culture.

Some training is needed simply in order to ensure conformity to the law or to the discipline of the Church. 'Equality and diversity' and 'safe from harm' training, for example, not only helps in ensuring that the fresh expression of church is a 'safe' expression of church, but also helps to safeguard the pioneer from potentially catastrophic litigation later. Pioneer ministry often involves being with those who are on the margins of society: the vulnerable and the weak in particular deserve the respect that is accorded to them when a pioneer has taken the trouble to be properly trained in how best to minister to them. Conducting a pioneer ministry to those who suffer from mental health problems or who are survivors of sexual abuse for example without first being trained in determining and setting appropriate pastoral boundaries could be life-threatening rather than life-enhancing for the very people it is intended to serve. A pioneer who chooses to ignore the fact that some parts of society are fractured and fragmented, often sick and perverted, violent and agitated, can hardly be said to communicate the love of God.

Christ's response to the temptation to throw himself off the highest building is a scriptural reminder to not put God to the test. When ministers stumble and fall it is all too often those whom they were ministering to, the vulnerable and the weak, who feel the pain of their brokenness the most. Good training and thorough preparation can safeguard against such hurt and damage. Far from being a denial of the power or grace of God to protect or save, pioneer training is thus an affirmation of God's determination to reach out to all people in love. The knowledge gained complements God's grace, enabling pioneers to work within their God-given abilities while accepting the invitation to develop and extend them. Those who persist in believing that God can equip pioneers with everything necessary for their ministry could do well to think about the fact that, by the grace of God, the Church has been able to ensure that appropriate training courses are available the length and breadth of the country. God does indeed provide!

Pioneering gifts and charisms

The seemingly endless range of gifts and charisms needed to support the practical skill set of a pioneer minister can be helpfully categorized as:

- Devotional
- Evangelical
- Incarnational.

Devotional

All pioneer ministry begins and ends in God. The great longing for God and for the kingdom of God is the gift of God and the source of all other charisms. It is vital, however, not to confuse this longing for God and the people of God with a deep-seated frustration with the state of the Church. The feeling that the Church is failing this generation, that it no longer reaches out (if it ever did) to the world in love and compassion may be justified. Longing for the Church to be different, however, is not the same as longing for God. Pioneer ministry is not rooted in God's love for the Church but in God's love for the world. The distinction is crucial and often is the only thing that prevents the pioneer from trying to be God and fix the Church rather than seeking to be with God and so build up the body of Christ. As Reginald Bibby stated recently:

> God . . . is not in trouble if people in a secular world stop going to church! God, in fact, is never in trouble at all.[25]

Pioneers who are more concerned with the state of the Church than they are with the love of God will never be able to create a fresh expression of church worthy of the name. Such communities are inevitably founded on irritation and frustration rather than grace and generosity of spirit. As hard as it might seem, God loves the Church as much as God loves those who are not yet a part of it and/or those who are called to expand and transform it. The first and most notable charism therefore of a pioneer minister is a devotion to God which engenders a positive compassion for God's people and which is evident in and through a relationship with the Church. This devotional charism expresses itself through prayer, adoration, worship and praise.

Pioneers have the gift of transforming what might seem to some to be a desperate situation or a mediocre existence into an opportunity or occasion for prayer: through their own communication with God, prayer becomes something tangible, real and effective rather than simply spoken or rehearsed. Similarly, life's joys, tears, opportunities and endings become moments of adoration when God is recognized in majesty and power, awe and wonder, joy and delight. The worship that results from the pioneer's own deep longing for God to be known and present in the world is not a weekly or daily rhythm of sitting, standing, singing and listening, but a full participation in the rhythm of life, the lives of others and the life of the world. It is the experience of this that enables the pioneer to identify and empathize with the longing and the need for God in others, and so reach out in God-given grace to minister God's love.

Evangelical

Pioneer ministry is all about sharing and communicating the good news of Christ and the kingdom. While it is true that not all evangelists are called to be pioneer ministers, by definition, all pioneer ministers will evangelize. Fresh ways of being church are nothing less than fresh ways of communicating the story of God and of God's love to those who are living in ignorance of their own part in the story. The way in which Philip was able to explain the Scriptures to the eunuch or Peter to Cornelius is a clear example of the sort of charism necessary. But precisely because God's story and the story of the listener are so intricately woven together, a simple regular recitation of the story will not do. God's story is always proclaimed – that is, told in such a way that it is real and transformative. On hearing the truth proclaimed, both the eunuch and later Cornelius were baptized. Truth, they discovered, is an encounter with Christ, not a fact to be narrated. The gift of communicating so that others are able to recognize the real and present truth of Christ while standing in a bus shelter, mashing up in a squat, meeting in a church hall, or lounging in a community centre or friend's home is not the gift of rhetoric or of clear speaking, but of evangelism.

> It was in an inner-city community centre and church where this 'thing' started, I call it a thing because I'm not sure really what it was, or what it is now, people call it a fresh expression of church; I just thought it was people living, loving and encountering God where God had previously been hidden from them.[26]

Incarnational

Although anthropologists and social scientists like to claim that humans are pack animals, few people seem able to run with the pack, or be at ease in community or even be comfortable standing alongside a neighbour. The ability to be 'present' to a group as one who is 'pre-sent' by God to communicate the gospel is a real charism. Incarnational charisms include those gifts that allow the pioneer to become a part of and to centre a community around the truth of God's love. They include the ability to engender a sense of purposeful belonging where formerly there was only attendance. The image of the lone pioneer may be romantic, but it is neither scriptural nor practical. Jesus was clearly unique in his calling yet he chose to surround himself with disciples whom he later called friends. 'You did not choose me, but I chose you.' Jesus chose to share the future plans for the kingdom with his friends, even though they were incapable of understanding or realizing the full extent of them. Paul, who is often described as the great pioneer of the gospel, also shared his ministry and outreach for the gospel. Apart from when he was in prison (and even here there are hints that he was seldom alone), Paul never practised ministry unaided. He travelled with Barnabas, John Mark, Silas, Timothy and Titus to name but a few. One of the reasons that Paul wrote his letters was to maintain his contact with the early church pioneers who were building on the foundations that God had laid through his shared ministry with them. The reluctance to share a vision or a call to pioneer ministry with others is often deeply rooted in a fear of opposition and of being misunderstood by the Church. Although, anecdotally, such fears might seem to be well founded, any cursory study of the history of the Church will prove otherwise.

The real danger to the gospel tends not to come from the Church inadvertently stifling fresh expressions of ministry, but from pioneers who insist on trying to work alone. Individuals who are convinced that God has given them, and them alone, the incarnational gifts and graces necessary to translate a vision of how a specific part of God's kingdom could be built are hardly the best people to model a Trinitarian God of loving relationships. On the other hand, confronting fear and ridicule, and taking risks for the sake of the good news is exactly what Christ expects and asks for in the model of incarnational ministry which he offers. The ability to gather together in order to build one another up in love, to share a vision, purpose and any practical insights into the work that God is calling people to do, lies at the heart of what it means to be a pioneer minister of the Church, regardless of how church is expressed.

2

Preparing

Pioneer ministry is part of the *Missio Dei*. It does not therefore happen by chance; neither can it achieve its full potential without considerable foresight, planning and preparation. The parables that Jesus tells to explain his ministry and the extent to which his coming and his ministry were prophesied in the Old Testament are compelling evidence of the extent of the divine forethought, preparation and planning that lie behind God's ministry of repentance and reconciliation. Only when all was prepared, in the fullness of time, did Christ come to his own. Then, as now, the ministry of reconciliation was and is too important to be left to chance. Pioneer ministry is a continuation of that same ministry of reconciliation. Although 'it can seem as though much that happens in Pioneer ministry is ad hoc and not "officially" planned',[1] the reality is that nothing could be further from the truth.

Planning helps to locate the ministry of the pioneer within the wider context of the *Missio Dei*. It can help pioneers to know where the boundaries of their ministry and their lines of accountability are. In spite of how it might seem at times, pioneers are not called to plan or prepare the *Missio Dei*. They are called only to participate in their particular part of it. The *Missio Dei* remains at all times the mission of God, not of the Church, its members, or its ministers. The difference is important. Ministry is not what we do, but is that which is

> determined and set forth by God's own ministry of revelation and reconciliation in the world, beginning with Israel and culminating in Jesus Christ and the Church.[2]

All planning and preparation for it should therefore be focused on enabling the pioneer to work *with* God not *for* God (as though God has no part in it). This, and this alone, is what makes the task of pioneering achievable and manageable. Being aware of human limitations while remaining open to the power of the Holy Spirit is the key.

Jesus proclaimed the good news, healed the sick and raised the dead. He also spent three years teaching and preparing his disciples how to be able to do the same after he had left. The twelve that Jesus called specifically to share in the ministry of reconciliation were given teaching additional to that which was given to the crowds. They were also sent out to practise their future ministry. The preparation that the disciples underwent was personal and practical and was centred on obedience to the two great commandments:

> 'The first is, "Hear, O Israel: the Lord our God, the Lord is one; you shall love the Lord your God with all your heart, and with all your soul, and with all your mind, and with all your strength." The second is this, "You shall love your neighbour as yourself." There is no other commandment greater than these.'
>
> (Mark 12.29–31)

Anyone contemplating participating in the pioneering work of the kingdom needs similar personal and practical preparation. The rest of this chapter therefore explores how obedience to the two great commandments still provides the best preparation for pioneering ministry.

Love God

There is no point to a pioneer ministry which is not grounded in a love of God. The first and greatest risk to pioneer ministry is that the minister, or the fledgling community, or even the Church, replaces God as the primary focus. The whole rationale for pioneer ministry is the 'love of God and to make disciples of Jesus Christ'. If you love me, says Christ, you will keep my commandments, the first of which is to love God. Only in their love for God will pioneers be able to discover the full potential of their ministry. It is out of their love for God that they will become aware of the height and breadth and depth of love necessary to minister effectively to God's people. History repeatedly shows that it is only when ministry is undertaken in obedience to the first commandment 'To love the Lord your God with all your heart and soul and strength' does obedience to the second commandment 'To love your neighbour as yourself' lead to God's kingdom being built, rather than some human parody of what is possible by grace.

Christ, who came 'full of grace and truth', is the link between grace and the pioneer's permission to share in the mission of God. It was through his perfect obedience and complete love of God that Christ was able to minister to the needs of the world, to bring healing and hope, truth and life. Ministry that is a response to Christ's call to discipleship and which is rooted in the ministry of Christ is a gift of grace (Rom. 12.6). Without this grace it is not possible to build up the body of Christ, and lead people to the truth of God in such a way that they are able to be a Christian community – a fresh expression of church.

The only proven Christlike way, therefore, of preparing for and sustaining a pioneer ministry which is part of the *Missio Dei* is by calling on and utilizing the means of grace. These are usually summarized as prayer, searching the Scriptures, sharing in Christian fellowship, receiving the Eucharist, and attending worship. By making use of these means of grace, pioneers are reminded of the importance and purpose of their calling and are renewed in their commitment to share in God's ministry.

Prayer

> He said to them, 'The harvest is plentiful, but the labourers are few; therefore ask the Lord of the harvest to send out labourers into his harvest.' (Luke 10.2)

If pioneers really want to help to bring in the harvest then they have to begin as Christ suggests – in prayer. They have to ask God for workers and trust that they are among those who form a part of God's answer to the prayer. Such prayer releases the potential of ministry by keeping it focused on the will of God. Prayer locates the ministry in God's intent instead of in the middle of human wants and needs or the pressing demands of the community. No ministry was arguably more pressing than that of Christ, yet Jesus also beseeched God. Jesus lived his whole life as an act of devotion and obedience to God, and taught and stressed to his disciples the importance of doing the same. His life of prayer was so remarkable that all four of the Gospel writers commented on it. Jesus didn't only pray at the appointed times and in the appointed places, he took time out to be by himself to pray. The more crowds gathered, the more Jesus took himself off alone to pray (Luke 5.15–16).

Sometimes the pioneer can be overwhelmed by the sheer size of the task to be done and lose the focus of the ministry as a result. By repeatedly offering the ministry back to God and seeking to discern God's will in it, the pioneer is reminded whose mission the ministry is a part of, and what its ultimate goal is.

To the crowds and Pharisees alike, Jesus was recognizable as a 'man of God' not just by the signs and wonders that he performed, but also by his devotional practices. It should be possible to say the same of every pioneer minister. Pioneers need to be praying ministers, deliberately, resolutely and visibly spending time with God praying for discernment and strength so that they are able to undertake the work that God has called them to. This should be more than a hurried prayer on the hoof, or casual conversation with God, this should be time committed to listening to and resting in the presence of God. The prayer life of a pioneer should be the source of his or her strength in the same way that it clearly was for Jesus while here on earth.

Prayer as anything other than a last resort has largely disappeared from modern life and most people are now so unfamiliar with the language of prayer that they are reluctant to pray openly either for themselves or for others. The increasing use of liturgical prayer in church has further exacerbated this situation by giving people the impression that the language of prayer needs to be learned and spoken in a particular format in order to be effective. Pioneers need to be unashamed and unafraid to be seen praying in public. With Jesus as their example, they should be so comfortable in prayer that they would be comfortable teaching others to pray if they are asked to. A prayerful pioneer ministry could help to reclaim the gift of prayer for the people of God in much the same way as the gift of 'The Lord's Prayer', with its almost scandalously familiar beginning 'Our Father', did for the first disciples of Jesus.

Christian conferring

Pioneers are called to minister to a culture that is predominantly post-Christian, and also post-atheist. It is not that people don't believe in God, they simply don't think God – or the Church – is important or worth considering. The Church is seen as irrelevant with nothing to say about the things that really concern people. Whether or not everyone has a 'God-shaped hole', the reality is that more people are concerned with the hole in the ozone layer than they are about either God or the Church. Earning enough to make ends meet in a time of recession, getting the children into good schools, paying the mortgage, keeping up the pension plan, all these things matter more to the largest section of the population than whether or not there is a God or whether they should go to church. Telling people that 'God loves them' without relating the significance of that statement to the very real everyday concerns that people have only serves to reinforce the general impression of the Church as out of step with modern life.

> There's no strategy, plan, or super slick method for bringing people into church or growing new churches, there's no label – pioneer or other – which will be the salvation of the Church, rather we fail to draw people into the divine dance and the human journey because we have become afraid to speak of faith as a normal part of our ordinary lives – faith has become either hidden, or extreme, or lost in church-ianity. We need to start making friends, drinking tea and chatting.[3]

Jesus spoke to the people of God, using stories and in language which made the message of the kingdom both relevant and accessible. His message was scriptural *and* contemporary. He frequently quoted from the Old Testament, from the Psalms and the prophets to explain the purpose of his ministry on earth and to explain its relevance to those he addressed. He told stories using images that were meaningful to his listeners and characters that they could empathize with. He interpreted the moral teachings in the books of the law and taught his disciples and the crowds how they should be applied.

Adapting the good news so that it can be communicated accurately and people can be ministered to effectively is not easy, but can be very rewarding in ministry. Paul's epistles, especially those written to the Church at Corinth and Galatia, make this all too evident. They should be compulsory reading for anyone looking to cross-cultural boundaries with the gospel. As Paul very quickly discovered, it is not possible to 'just tell people about Jesus'. Before too long he found he was embroiled in questions about circumcision, idols, the Eucharist, immorality, the law, baptism, life after death, the place of women, the proper use of money, and so on.

Most forms of pioneer ministry and fresh expressions of church initiated outside the Church are based around a model of Christian conferring as a means of grace. By simply engaging people in conversation that is relevant to them, enabling them to recognize the way in which the gospel speaks into their current situation, Christian community is formed. Café Church in Starbucks is one obvious example of this, as is Pub-Pews, a fresh expression of church which began life as a group of Christian graduates who shared a pint with their friends in a local pub once a week on a Tuesday evening and tried to put the world to rights using only ideas taken from the Gospels. Invited friends, or members of the local, were allowed to raise any issue from that day's newspapers, which was then debated using the Gospels as though the issue was being put to Jesus. The question they asked was 'What does Jesus say?'

The potential for pioneering that comes from Christian conferring is phenomenal. The risk, as always, is that pioneers will assume that they have to have all the answers! As a means of grace, however, Christian conferring is as much about listening as it is about speaking. Personal testimony is a powerful evangelistic tool and can also be a profoundly humbling invitation to the pioneer to listen once again to the call of God on people's lives. Including time to listen and time to share what God has already done and how God is already at work in the life of the community anchors a pioneer ministry or fresh expression of church in the love of God. One pioneer ministry, for example, which functioned as a Christian book club, initially attracted a great deal of interest. Around 30 people gathered fortnightly to discuss a book, which was deliberately chosen in order to encourage interest in matters of faith, without being deliberately 'religious'. Over a relatively short period of time, however, the numbers began to decline until they were down to the regular 10 or 12. The conversation was good, but it never moved past the book in the way that the originators had hoped, until someone was brave enough to suggest that they include a slot at the end to ask for testimony. People were invited to give an opinion not just on the book, but on how the book reflected something of their own faith journey. The person was then prayed for by the rest of the group. Once the conversation moved out of the realm of fiction and focused on the facts of people's lives God became something that people found they could converse with one another about. The group recently made a choice to alternate between novels and books of the Bible, or great Christian classics as a result of their growing interest in God.

All conversation, but especially that which is deliberately focused on the work of God, can be used by the Holy Spirit to speak, and be heard, in the different languages of contemporary culture.

Searching the Scriptures

When the great doctor of theology Karl Barth was asked by an elderly lady how he knew that Jesus loved him he is reputed to have answered in the words of the children's hymn, 'Jesus loves me, this I know, for the Bible tells me so.' It is through their study of the Scriptures that pioneers are able to know and grow in the love of God which they believe they are called to share with others. Jesus prepared his disciples for their ministry by opening up the Scriptures to them. According to Luke, following his resurrection, Jesus spent time with his disciples and 'Then he opened their minds to understand the scriptures' (Luke 24.45) and spoke to them 'about the kingdom of God' (Acts 1.3). The disciples and the Gospel writers then shared that understanding using the same methods that Jesus had used. The Gospel writers tried to communicate the good news of the coming kingdom in ways that spoke to the realities of people's lives. Mark presents Jesus as one, 'who although ultimately triumphant, nevertheless experiences isolation, alienation, lack of understanding, and suffering that climaxes in his cry on the cross. In Mark's Gospel the situation of Jesus is analogous to that of his community, who likewise knew the reality of persecution and suffering.'[4]

Even though Jesus chose different, challenging and 'fresh' ways of proclaiming the kingdom, such as teaching the crowd from boats, by the side of lakes, up mountains, and so on, he could never have been accused by the religious leaders of his day of 'dumbing-down' the message of the Scriptures. The Sermon on the Mount and his discussions with the scribes and Pharisees, as recorded in John's Gospel, challenged the scholarly and religious understanding of his time. They remind the Church and its ministers that the Scriptures are not easy to understand or to interpret: they need to be studied.

Pioneers often ask, 'Does the study of Scripture or theology really matter as long as someone comes to faith?' Yes. It can be soul-destroying and profoundly damaging to discover the very thing that led you to Christ is considered a dangerous lie or untruth by other Christians. Getting it right, knowing the difference between opinion and truth is important, for pioneers as well as for those they are trying to communicate the gospel to. The history of heresy runs side by side with the history of the Church as a record of just how frighteningly easy it is to make mistakes in such matters. It takes wisdom, skill and Spirit to adapt the work of God and serve the present age. The pioneer does not need to personally possess all three gifts, but does need to be able to gather together all three and know how to combine them.

Knowledge of Scripture and theology matter because it is impossible to know, speak of, to, about or with God without them. Anyone who says, 'Jesus saves', is speaking theologically; anyone who says, 'Jesus saves everyone unconditionally', is treading on dangerous ground. Unconditional grace and universalism are not accepted as Christian truths by all Christians. For this reason, as much as for their own deepening relationship with God, the Bishops' Guidelines for pioneer ministers state that pioneers need to be as immersed in the Scriptures as every other member of the priesthood. 'They also need specialist training in inculturation and cross cultural mission . . . Particular attention, we believe, needs to be paid to ecclesiology.'[5]

Worship and the sacraments of the Church

Love of God expresses itself in a desire to take seriously the call to holiness, to 'be holy' even as God is holy. It is in the worship and the sacraments of the Church that Christians are best enabled to do this, to become, for a short space of time, totally 'other', to become lost in wonder, love and praise. Sacrament inevitably ties grace down to recognizable forms of life and practice, ones to which God in Christ has made an incarnational commitment both in principle and in particular.[6] Regardless of how much thought and effort is expended on making a fresh expression of church 'meaningful' or 'contemporary', if there is no opportunity or means of worshipping God and receiving the sacrament of Holy Communion it will die for it will have no heart. Worship is how humans are called to express their love for God, and the celebration of the Eucharist is one of the primary means by which they receive the grace of God in return. Worship, however, cannot be commanded, no matter how urgent the need – it can only be participated in, for true worship only happens in the fullness of the presence of God. If God is not the centre of the sacrament all that is left are empty words.

Jesus knew the difference between devotion to God and religion, and recognized the value and importance of both. In spite of believing the Pharisees to be hypocrites, and in spite of his anger at the abuse of religion which led him to purge the temple forecourts with a whip made by his own hand, Jesus did not despise the Church of his time, but ministered within it where possible. He celebrated the major festivals in Jerusalem and went to the temple to pray and discuss the word of God. The Gospels narrate that Jesus attended synagogue regularly throughout his earthly ministry, not only when he was called upon to read and expound the Scriptures. All of which suggests that no matter how outdated or mistaken pioneers believe the traditional Church to be, or how angry or frustrated it makes them, it should still be recognized as the place appointed by God to receive the gifts of grace that will nourish and restore them in their work of ministering to others. Not least because it anchors their ministry and calling to a wider perspective of God's word. The story of Nicodemus serves as a reminder that their presence at the sacraments, and their contributions in Bible study, and at Christian fellowship, might help inspire others to question and explore.

Love your neighbour

Pioneer ministry is not done to the world, but with and for the world out of God's love for the world. The question 'Who is my neighbour?' has already been answered by Christ. It could however be argued that pioneer ministers are the equivalent to the good Samaritan, prepared to pick up those who have fallen along the way whom the Church either does not see, or is too afraid to engage with. Pioneers know that by the grace of God they are called to love the world, even with its moral inadequacies, and in its sometimes hostile attitude towards faith and religion. Nobody is excluded, everyone is included in the kingdom, but not everyone can 'get to Jericho' unscathed or without the help of a friend.

The hardest part for those who would begin a pioneer ministry is learning to love their neighbour by thinking outside of the box of the Church. Church people tend to think about people and mission in certain ways; their hopes and dreams are usually centred on the Church and what it is about the Church that they either approve or disapprove of. This way of thinking leads to trying to design 'new' or 'fresh' ways of having a one-hour 'God slot' somewhere in the week or the month which seeks to address the perceived shortcomings. A lack of children in the Church, for example, leads to the creation of some sort of 'youth service' or for more 'contemporary' worship. A desire to attract 'young families' turns into a 'family friendly' or 'all age' service on Saturday mornings, or a particular brand of fresh expression of church called 'Messy Church'[7] on Thursday afternoons. While not wanting to discourage such creative ventures, it is important to recognize that these are not pioneering ministries. They may be 'fresh expressions of church' but they are also 'in the box' projects, rooted in the (mistaken) idea that to really know God and be blessed by God, people should come to church.

A pioneering ministry modelled after Christ's own ministry does not start in the Church, but in the world. As Einstein said: 'We can't solve problems by using the same kind of thinking we used when we created them.' Instead of being in church and asking, 'What would make people want to come here?' start where the people are and ask, 'What does being church look like in this place?' God is already at work in the world and is issuing the Church an invitation to come and share. Real love of neighbours is expressed by a willingness to join with them wherever they are rather than simply dictate where they should be.

Thinking 'outside the box' is best done outside of the box; for this reason, pioneer ministry often begins by the pioneer simply being 'out and about', finding out where the people are that God is calling the Church to minister to and seeing what God is doing in that place.

At The Living Room at Southampton University, for example, there has been a deliberate attempt to create a place where students without a church background can go and discover the trans-forming power of Jesus. The format of the evening is designed specifically to cater for people who never normally go to church. Zoe Hart, one of the student workers, says: 'Our values are "loving God, loving each other and loving the lost", quite simple really: The Greatest Commandments and The Great Commission. These values shape everything we do.' The emphasis is on doing what students do, but doing it with God, being together, eating together, discussing together what really matters.

Although some pioneers can trace their calling to ministry back to a crystal clear vision from the Holy Spirit, it is also increasingly the case that the form or nature of their ministry is unknown until they respond to a more general calling to proclaim the kingdom wherever they are or until they have completed their research into the local community and into their own gifts and graces. This demands both sensitivity and skill in listening and discernment.

> A spiritual sensitivity to the places and ways in which the Lord of the harvest is working is crucial for anyone wanting to serve the Lord.[8]

To begin pioneering, look for the gathering places, the community spaces, the street corners, town centres, school gates, social networks, watering holes, blog spaces, leisure parks, and workplaces. Go to wherever people congregate, willingly or not, and see the neighbour there. Neil Cole puts it like this:

> When looking for a pocket of people, remember the saying that bad people make good soil – there's a lot of fertilizer in their lives.[9]

Spend time in these places, serving the needs of that community, listening, praying, listening, being present, listening and trying to see the church that is already there. By praying, serving and listening, find the key to unlock the particular contextual gift of ministry for that specific community.

It is in service to the community, in small but important and meaningful ways, that the pioneer is able to learn the language of the community and hear what the real needs of the people are and what God is saying about them.

> But we were gentle among you, like a nurse tenderly caring for her own children. So deeply do we care for you that we are determined to share with you not only the gospel of God but also our own selves, because you have become very dear to us.
>
> (1 Thess. 2.7b–8)

It is when the Christian is serving others out of love of neighbour that the gospel is at its most credible in today's sceptical society. The Bridge, for example, is a pioneering venture set up by the Church Army in London to cater for the practical and spiritual needs of the homeless. Richard Dadds says of its vision: 'The initial focus of our work is on developing authentic community, based on the Christian principles of loving and caring for every individual, regardless of their background or beliefs.'[10] In caring for the homeless, those at The Bridge seek to evangelize within the homeless community and are experimenting with forms of church that are perhaps more appropriate for those living and working in such communities.

As they serve, pioneers listen for and reflect on possible answers to the question: 'Where is God at work here and what part am I being asked to play?' According to Anderson,

> Theological reflection does not ask the question 'What would Jesus do in this situation?' because this question would imply his absence. Rather, it asks the question 'Where is Jesus in this situation and what am I to do as a minister?'[11]

Each specific ministry begins when the pioneer has prayerfully begun to discern an answer to that question. This is often achieved by imagining what an awareness of the presence of God might look like for the people of that community. It is prompted by questions such as, 'In what way would the community change?', 'How would it need to be different?', and even more importantly – how will 'church' need to be different and the communication of the gospel changed?

Learning love of neighbour means learning to contextualize a ministry, to ensure that it is something designed to meet the neighbour's needs. Contextualization can be understood as 'the dynamic process whereby the constant message of the gospel interacts with specific relative human situations'.[12] A contextualized ministry engages seriously with the local cultural context and presents Christianity in such a way that it meets the deepest needs of the people it is intended to reach and penetrates their worldviews so completely that it cannot possibly be deemed either irrelevant or foreign. According to Frost and Hirsch, to contextualize is to understand the language, longings, lifestyle patterns and worldview of our neighbours and to adjust our practices accordingly without compromising the gospel. This is something that takes time and effort – there is no short-cut.

The difference good contextualization can make to a fresh expression of church or pioneer ministry should not be underestimated. It is significant that Jesus 'came to his own' and that he urged the disciples to 'go first to the house of Israel' (Matt. 10.5). He sent the disciples out in pairs to towns and villages where they might expect to find a small community that might be receptive to the message he asked them to carry. Knowing the area, the people and the context and culture of the community well enough to be able to speak the gospel into that space for that time, is what fresh expression of church is all about.

> When I came to you, brothers and sisters, I did not come proclaiming the mystery of God to you in lofty words or wisdom. For I decided to know nothing among you except Jesus Christ, and him crucified. And I came to you in weakness and in fear and in much trembling. (1 Cor. 2.1–3)

According to national statistics, just under half of the population (46 per cent) said that they knew most or many people in their neighbourhood. More than half (58 per cent) felt they could trust most or many people in their neighbourhood.[13] The belief in the importance of community is apparently still strong enough in most neighbourhoods to enable a pioneer, willing to live and work in community, to become accepted and trusted. This is essential, as a minister needs to be 'in solidarity with the pains, hopes, fears and joys of the world before moving on to challenge that world from the point of view of the gospel and the cross'.[14]

> What's exciting to many parishes about Fresh Expressions is the flexibility it offers to devise ways to bring about more community cohesion. The Rev Ben Norton, 28, who is training to be a pioneer minister based in Bridlington, Yorkshire, started a Fresh Expressions for men aged between 18 and 40. They meet in a pub on Sunday nights to discuss the news in a Christian context and to arrange other events including paintballing and clay-pigeon shooting. He has 15 regulars and 20 part-timers. 'To open a Bible, or to openly pray together would be too much,' he said. 'This is first base engagement with spirituality.'[15]

Contextualized ministry attempts to make the body of Christ present and real to people wherever they are rather than expecting people to come to a specific time and place to meet with God (although that opportunity is not excluded). There are nonetheless two fundamental differences between Christ's incarnational ministry and the contextualized ministry of a pioneer. First, a pioneer minister is not God, but seeks to work with God. God is already present wherever a pioneer minister is 'sent'. The second difference follows on from the first: whereas Jesus could perfectly discern the will of God and accordingly knew where to go, what to say and how and when to act, the pioneer must depend on an imperfect ability corrected by the gift of the Holy Spirit, to discern the will of God. In spite of being so obvious, it can be frighteningly easy to lose sight of these differences in the grip of the God-given certainty, passion and zeal for the *Missio Dei* which is the hallmark of pioneers.

Pioneer ministry proclaims the coming kingdom of God and seeks to make God's presence known to those who, for whatever reason, do not yet know the meaning of Immanuel – God with us. This cannot be achieved through a mere statement of fact, however, even if that fact is interpreted into the language of the community. Scripture and the history of the Church and mission demonstrate that the knowledge of God is only made real through the proclamation of the gospel. The gospel is only proclaimed when it is told in such a way that it becomes real and present to those who hear it. When Christ proclaimed the kingdom was near, it was near to those who heard the message. Jesus proclaimed the good news to everyone who would listen in such a way that they could hear and recognize its relevance and claim on their lives. He taught crowds on mountain tops and devout Jews in the synagogues. He taught and preached from boats and in the temple courtyard. He spoke of food, of money, of taxes and of politics. He related the kingdom to the everyday life of those who thought that God was nothing to do with them, and helped them to make the connections. His is the model of accessible contextualized ministry that the pioneer needs to follow.

As part of the preparation for pioneer ministry therefore pioneers need to avoid generalizations and undertake whatever research is necessary to know and become a part of the community they are called to minister to. To repeat: this cannot be done from a distance, the pioneer needs to enter into the community, to prepare for the ministry by spending time – quality time, earning the trust and respect of the community, before daring to assume enough knowledge to proclaim what the community needs most. Frost and Hirsch liken such pioneers to 'soul whisperers', ministers who do for community what Monty Roberts did with horses. A soul whisperer is someone who will listen to the deepest longings of the community he or she is called to minister to and then try and engage with them with respect, grace and compassion.[16]

It is crucial that pioneer ministers are able to see the potential for ministry that God has created, whether in their imagination, in a vision or dream, or as a consequence of painstaking research. In seeing the potential for ministry, pioneers see both the presence of Christ and those whom Christ has sent them to minister to. Often, these people are more visible by their absence in the regular church or faith communities, than by their presence, for example children, the sick, the poor, drug addicts, prostitutes, the outcasts: the list hasn't changed much since Christ's time. Sometimes, however, the pioneer is led to recognize those within the Church who do not know God or who are not in community with the people of God.

Love yourself

Pioneers are important to God, not because they are pioneers, but because they too are children of God, in need of God's love, care and compassion, forgiveness and reconciliation. The ministry that pioneers model by the way in which they live their lives and take care of themselves says more about their real conviction of God's love than words ever will.

Pioneering is difficult, demanding and risky work, often undertaken well away from the usual comfort zones of belonging that provide support for church ministry. Because of this, pioneers need to develop a personal strength and resilience that is fed directly from their relationship with Jesus rather than from the community. Dependence on Christ rather than on the Church is not an easy skill to learn, however, as it entails a degree of personal accountability which is all too easy to avoid as a part of the community of the faithful. St Peter's personal preparation, for example, included learning what it meant to love Christ in spite of personal weaknesses rather than simply to confess Christ as

Messiah. Saul similarly needed to learn what it was to be terribly blind to the truth, albeit zealously well intentioned for God, before he could pioneer his ministry to the Gentiles. Church history relates how a significant number of the disciples and early pioneers of the kingdom were prepared for their ministry by first confronting their weakness or whatever it was that they feared most. Learning humility before God, and being able to acknowledge that commitment, good intentions and zeal are not enough, is essential for all Christians, but it is especially needed by those who are called to pioneer new initiatives or fresh expressions of church. The extent to which personal charisms are emphasized in a significant number of fresh expressions, emergent churches and pioneer ministries is difficult to reconcile with the fact that all ministry, if it is of God, is communal and intended for the building up of the whole body of Christ.

The pressure on a pioneer minister to be 'up-front', 'creative', 'innovative' and charismatic should not be underestimated, neither should the all-too-human longing to succeed, achieve and be liked. These two can combine with disastrous consequences to create pioneers who come to believe that they, and they alone, can do the work that God needs to be done, or worse, ministers who prostitute their God-given calling in a desperate need to be seen as a pioneer or an innovator. The cult of the individual is as endemic in the Church as it is in society, and it is not difficult for someone doing something radical or different to attain a following. It is in this context that Paul's admonition to the Corinthians over whose disciples they are should be read:

> My brothers, some from Chloe's household have informed me that there are quarrels among you. What I mean is this: One of you says, 'I follow Paul'; another, 'I follow Apollos'; another, 'I follow Cephas'; still another, 'I follow Christ.'

Paul goes on to ask them

> Is Christ divided? Was Paul crucified for you? Were you baptised into the name of Paul?   (1 Cor. 1.11–13, NIV)

One pioneer minister spoke of how after months of careful preparation and good advertising, he held his first pioneering 'service' in a warehouse. It was packed to overflowing with people who had come to support him, to see what he was doing, to try this new thing that they had heard about. After what he thought was a great service, he couldn't resist commenting to a retired priest who had stood quietly throughout the service at the back – 'I bet you never pack them in your church like this.' 'No, young man,' came the dry reply, 'but then, these people came here to see you, they come to the church to see God.' Good pioneering initiatives will always draw people's attention to God, not the minister.

Hauerwas and Willimon provide a harsh warning for those who do not take seriously the consequences of ministers liking to be liked and needing to be needed. Ministers frequently underestimate the depth and extent of the needs of those that they have committed themselves to minister to.

> One day they may awake to find that they have sacrificed family, self-esteem, health and happiness for a bunch of selfish people who have eaten them alive. Pastors then come to despise what they are and to hate the community that made them that way.[17]

The truth is, of course, that it was their own need to be liked and wanted that made them that way, not the needs of others, they simply didn't see it. Personal preparation for ministry must therefore always include regular periods of self-examination and ministerial accountability when questions such as 'Why do I need to do what I am doing?' and 'How does this serve the purpose of God?' are asked with complete honesty and candour and offered to God in prayer and devotion.

Often it is only through such reflection that people are led to recognize the limitations of their calling. Being the person who saw the potential for the ministry, who dreamed of it and who cares passionately about it, does not necessarily mean that one is the right person to undertake the ministry. God may have given the vision to one, and equipped someone else with the necessary gifts and graces to implement or practise it. Both John the Baptist and Jesus were essential to the *Missio Dei*, but John was not the Messiah. For the dreamer, the would-be pioneer, this can be bitterly hard to accept, but it is essential that such knowledge come to the fore sooner rather than later. Pioneer ministry is hard enough when someone has been equipped by God with the gifts and graces necessary to undertake it. It can be very bruising and damaging to both the individual and those towards whom the ministry is directed if it is attempted by someone without the necessary charisms.

It is a sad reflection of society's impact on the Church that a few of those who discovered late in the process that they were not equipped by God for pioneer ministry reported being made to feel somehow 'second best' when they asked to be transferred to a more traditional form of ministry. Nonetheless, without exception they felt justified in their decisions, and thankful for having had the opportunity to explore their ministry and test their call.

The prayer of Jesus in the Garden of Gethsemane is worth reading regularly as the prayer of a pioneering minister.

> Father, if you are willing, remove this cup from me; yet, not my will but yours be done. (Luke 22.42)

Every pioneer should regularly consider how to react to the idea of God responding, 'I will take the cup of your pioneering ministry away from you – and give it to another.'

3

Pioneering

Sharing in the *Missio Dei* is an exciting and life-changing experience, which means it can also be very unnerving. Everything is different, for, as God promises, my ways are not your ways and 'new' really does mean 'new', not rehashed, remodelled, or even re-created.

There are usually five common components to planting a fresh expression or starting a pioneer ministry, which need not necessarily happen in sequential order but which, when the pattern is established, tend to be cyclical. An easy way of remembering them is to think of GRACE:

- Gather support
- Rehearse the message
- Aspire to greatness
- Communicate the vision
- Expect success.

Gather support

Almost the first thing that Christ did in his earthly ministry was to call together the disciples, those who would journey with him to Jerusalem, sharing bread, hearing the mission, feeding back reactions, and so on. Even though the disciples had been waiting, perhaps even longing for the Messiah to arrive, they still needed to be invited to share in the mission. The same is true in pioneer ministry. There may well be more people in the Church longing and waiting for something to happen than the pioneer knows of, but they will need to be invited to share. How they are invited will depend on the pioneer, but meeting in cyberspace, social networks, via Christian blogs and through virtual churches can be every bit as effective as meeting after the service on a Sunday night or in a café on the high street. As with Jesus and the selection of his disciples, what matters is not where or how, but why and with whom.

There is a reason for the invitation. People are being selected and invited to share in the discernment of God's will, to assist in God's ministry. The invitation to meet and discuss ministry is a form of Christian conferring and is a means of grace. It provides an opportunity for God's Spirit to be heard and responded to. Wherever possible, at least one person should be selected who will have agreed oversight of the pioneer, someone who is aware of the dangers as well as the rewards of pioneer ministry, who knows when it is time to rest, and when it is time to push on. Likewise, someone other than the pioneer with direct knowledge or experience of the people for whom the ministry is intended should also be included. For example, if the ministry is intended to reach out to unchurched pensioners from a nearby residential care home then the gathering would benefit from listening first to the contributions of someone who has worked with the elderly. This person need not be a church member, or even a Christian. What matters is the opportunity to listen to that perspective. Seeking expert advice is extremely helpful in unmasking false presumptions. Perhaps the 'poor lonely old folk' in question are not as poor or as lonely as the group might have first presumed them to be.

It is also important to include people who share the same aims and objectives as the pioneer, who can act as a sounding-board for the plans. God does not only speak to and through the pioneer. If a similar project is already under way elsewhere, it is always worth inviting those engaged in it to come and speak to the fledgling ministry. Even though no two ministries are ever the same it is usually very helpful to listen to what worked and what didn't for another group. Every effort should be made to ensure that the invitation is open to anyone God might be trying to invite into the conversation, not just the people who immediately spring to mind. As well as inviting those who it may be supposed would be supportive of the idea, a way should be found of including in the growing group at least one or two people whose opinion is valued, not because they would necessarily agree with the project on principle, but because it is known that they have the courage and ability to speak the truth as they are given it.

Lastly, it is essential to gather support from among the community or group that the ministry is intended to serve. The Church has suffered from far too many 'youth services' prepared by those who have no idea what it is to be a young person today, or from family-friendly services designed and prepared without a thought for crèches or for what it takes to get four children all under ten ready to leave the house by 9.30 in the morning! Whether the ministry is intended for young or old, for rich or poor, it cannot be done 'to' them, only with them as Christ's incarnational ministry demonstrates.

If the intended ministry is of God, then as it grows it can be expected to gather together a startling variety of people. The contrary voice provides an important, some would say an essential, balance to every pioneer ministry group. It serves as a reminder that all ministries should be open and inclusive and that it should expect to meet with reasonable opposition. Contrary voices are often the only means that pioneers have in the early days of hearing an alternative perspective or theological corrective to their ministerial intent. They should be honestly welcomed and recognized as those who also seek to serve God with integrity. Interestingly, it is known that such people often become the fiercest supporters of the pioneer and of the new ministry. As the selection of the twelve disciples of Jesus proved, the only thing that all the supporters of a pioneer ministry tend to have in common is the good news.

The primary purpose of the group is to listen, to reflect and to listen again. They help by testing the ideas suggested by the pioneer against what is already known and believed, and then listening again for the voice of God and the call of Christ in them. They feed back to the pioneer what others are saying in response to the ministry and help to keep everyone focused on the goal.

even pioneers like Barnabas and Paul will sometimes need, for the sake of God's mission, to invest the necessary time in meetings and councils of various kinds. There will be forms to fill in, papers to write, budgets to prepare and orders to draft summarising decisions which have been made. It may not feel like the most congenial or constructive type of activity . . . But it is a necessary and important part of God's mission.[1]

Recording meetings in some way, either using a tape recorder or through someone taking minutes, sounds terribly formal, but there is often no other way of holding on to those things that merit further reflection later. Meetings should be kept to a minimum, and it should be agreed beforehand what will be expected of each person so that it is clear how often each one's presence will be required and in what capacity. Taking part in an uncertain, experimental project in an advisory capacity and doing so as a decision-maker are two very different tasks. As a rough guide, the size of the regular group should be no more than ten or twelve and, in the early stages of the project, the group should expect to meet once for every four or five 'ministry moments': for example, once a week for a project that has daily contact, or once a quarter for a project that only takes place every three or four weeks.

It helps to remind the whole group of the listening brief of such meetings if they begin with a short act of worship which includes prayer for the project and for the pioneer minister as well as for the work of the group.

Rehearse the message

Practice makes perfect – and pioneer ministry needs repeated rehearsing in order to be genuinely responsive and spontaneous as well as effective. Everyone encounters the opportunity to be spontaneous at some time in their ministry, but it takes practice to be able to turn spontaneity into an effective ministry for Christ. Jesus prepared the disciples for their future ministry by sending them out to rehearse a ministry of proclamation long before they could possibly have understood what it was all about. It was three years later, at least, before his death and resurrection made them realize the importance of that lesson. Requiring them to do in some small way while he was with them what they would have to do later after his ascension was one of the key means by which Jesus released the gifts and graces of the disciples to build up the Church. Similarly, rehearsing what is intended in pioneer ministry not only helps to test if the ministry is of God, but also provides invaluable experience for later.

Try it. Just give it a go. The best advice is to get on and do it. Rehearsing doesn't mean not really doing it. To rehearse the message means doing it in such a way that it can be learned from and improved on next time. When the disciples were sent out the first time, it was a real ministry in its own right – 'The seventy returned with joy, saying, "Lord, in your name even the demons submit to us!"' (Luke 10.17). In the same way, larger projects or fresh expressions of church can usually be broken down into smaller, semi-independent stages, each of which can be rehearsed separately. In addition to providing much-needed feedback on the effectiveness or otherwise of the intended ministry, rehearsals usually provide the information necessary for realistic resource requirements and costings to be determined. David Warnock suggests:

> Try things. Don't worry about failure (after all that is certain if you do nothing). Try things in a simple, cheap, prototyping way to see what will work. What does work will surprise you.[2]

Trying out what is possible first is often skipped by pioneers keen to start their ministry. Just because something is possible, however, does not always mean it is completely practical from the onset.

> We are told in the New Testament to count the cost before beginning something new. Sometimes it will be the right answer to count that cost and then say, always with regret, we simply can't begin this at the moment.[3]

Rehearsing a fresh expression, that is starting it with a view to being able to learn from it and adapt it, means that people are less likely to give up when things go wrong – as they often do. God asks for participation not perfection.

Shena Woolridge for example wrote that in Easter 2008 her church decided to run a family-friendly café church. The event was a great success with every table full (about 30 people in all).

One practical difficulty was identified. 'I didn't have adequate amplification on the DVD and for me as I tried to lead the service in this environment.' But the group received confirmation about the level of staffing they had decided on: 'We had 5 team members and needed every one of them!' They also received some 'very positive feedback', which made them 'want to endeavour to put on one service a month'.[4]

Sometimes rehearsing provides the confidence needed to persuade a group to 'go for it!'. This was the case for Lucie and Richard Clarkson and the youth service they were part of. 'We spent a long time planning and praying about how to do it and what sort of thing to do but weren't really sure what we should be doing. In September, after a few trial services, we just decided to start it and see how it went so we began a weekly meeting/bible study.'[5]

In the above examples, there was little that needed to be adapted in the light of the practice projects. There are times, however, when it can be important to refine even well tried and trusted approaches such as home churches, Alpha and Start![6] according to the specific context of the ministry.

Ian and Erika Biscoe for example needed to adapt the church that they formed at the prompting of a member of the community:

> Jane lives next door to the base house we moved into. She began asking us when were we going to start church! That wasn't really our idea, so in the first months of arriving, we started a meeting in our home. Jane and another guy quickly became Christians. A number of other folk came to these Sundays in our home, but we noticed they only ever came once. This led us to explore the social patterns on the estate. People didn't invite one another into their homes – they talk on the doorstep. So we saw that church in the home wasn't so appropriate in this culture.[7]

Similarly, when Duncan and Ann Petty planted a new church in an Urban Priority Area they tried to run Start! courses before people were ready for them, and, in their own words, 'they duly flopped'. On reflection, they realized that more time was needed building trust in this particular context than they had allowed for: 'although we ran loads of things to do this e.g. cruise evenings, environmental clean-ups, Easter Egg hunts, BBQ's and the like we still tried to move too fast'.

Duncan and Ann's experience also taught them the importance of rehearsals in reclaiming the focus of their ministry. When reflecting on what they could learn from their very successful ministry planting a new church, they listed leaning on their own ideas rather than God's ideas too much as the most significant thing that they did wrong. 'It is so easy to be enthusiastic in this and to run away with your initiatives instead of looking for what the Spirit is up to and going with that.'[8] Rehearsing not only helps to resolve practical issues such as sound systems, the numbers of chairs needed, getting the right permissions from the local authorities, and so on, it also provides the prospective pioneer and all those involved with much-needed feedback on the nature of the calling and on the gifting needed for the ministry. This information forms the basis for the theological and spiritual reflection necessary to discern whether or not the ministry is both viable and fit for purpose or needs to be modified.

Aspire to greatness

It is surprising how limited and small some visions for pioneer ministry are. Often this is for no other reason than that people have been trained by the current church climate to think small. Churches are limited spaces, even cathedrals and mega-churches have a limit on the number of people who can sit down to worship at any one time. The kingdom however is not limited to the number of people who can worship at a single sitting, neither is it confined to a building. Pioneer ministry should not therefore be limited in its scope to the number of people or chairs in a church. The kingdom spans all of creation, and the joy of pioneer ministry is the freedom that it grants to every minister to claim, as Wesley did, 'The world is my parish.' The mandate from Jesus is: 'Go therefore and make disciples of all nations' (Matt. 28.19). Pioneers are asked by God to aspire to greatness, to minister to the whole world, rather than to a specific congregation. Although they may begin by discerning the needs of this or that specific community, the vision that they are given is seldom confined to that. In the best pioneering spirit, they are able to see how their ideas and insights into the kingdom can be developed and grown outside of their originating context.

This is an important difference between pioneering initiatives and traditional church planting. Church planting is a means of growing the Church by taking what already exists and repro-ducing it elsewhere. The vision is of church rather than kingdom, of services and worship, structures and offices rather than of communities and networks of relationships. The idea behind church plants is that creation is somehow divided into the Church and the rest of the world. People are therefore thought of as either churched or unchurched. Pioneer ministry, on the other hand, is a means of growing relationships, in particular, the relationship between God and the people of God. As every person is a child of God, and hence in a relationship with God (whether knowingly or not) it is not possible to think of 'in' or 'out', or even 'lost' or 'found' in the same way.

Pioneers are called to see the potential for kingdom commun-ity in the networks and relationships that already exist, but which are often ignored or undervalued in terms of their contribution to gospel values or human well-being. Many of these relationships are forged out of necessity rather than choice but this does not mean that the networks they create are not potential kingdom communities. High street chaplains, for example, often comment that community relationships can be formed out of nothing more tangible than the fact that all those involved work in the same shopping precinct and are forced to share the same amen-ities. Similarly, '37' in south-east England attempts to release the kingdom potential in the relationships formed by people who regularly travel on the number 37 bus. They are bound together by nothing more substantial than the fact that they journey together. Normally conversation between passengers is rare and happens only in response to shared provocation such as the bus being late, cancelled, or full. Yet over the course of time, the passengers can end up spending several hours together a month. By doing nothing more than travelling with them, initiating and encouraging conversation, noticing who is missing and who is new from one week to the next, and so promoting other passengers to communicate with each other, one pioneer minister regularly transforms a community of necessity into a kingdom community of care and concern. 'Their worship is their fellowship, their prayer is the "God Bless" that they now call out to me and each other as they get off at their stop, their sacrament is the sacrament of care, what more does a church need?' The dream is of the day when all local bus services are recognized as more than just transport services.

Contemporary community is not always easy to recognize, however, as twenty-first-century relationships can be very diverse. Some, for example, exist only in the virtual world of Second Life or similar social networking sites on the internet. This does not make the relationships or community that they engender any less real, or less kingdom. It merely makes it a little harder to predict what a fully formed community or network of such relationships would look like as 'church'. This is not a problem, as aspiring to greatness for the kingdom requires that imagination combined with vision and hope are united to risk, rather than that predictable outcomes are married to known statistical data. Einstein is reputed to have said, 'Imagination is more important than knowledge.' In the case of pioneer ministry, this is definitely true.

Aspiring to greatness means being open to the vision that God has and setting goals for ministry that lie outside of what would normally be dreamed of. It entails having an imagination that sees the gospel not as a three-point sermon, but as an ongoing conversation complete with body language, and the potential for heated discussion. Aspiring to greatness means seeing the Eucharist not in small glasses or silver chalices of wine, but in street parties, luncheon clubs, water stations and soup kitchens. It means learning how to honour a baptism where tears are the water and the promises are to stop self-harm, put away the needles and live! It means learning to sing a new song in a strange land where street rap and dance are recognized as worship and clubbing as church. Aspiring to greatness is about imagining a relationship with God that everyone can participate in, including those who can't sing, can't read and won't sit still.

Communicate the vision

Religion is no longer a private affair. The twentieth-century obsession with privacy of faith was the first casualty in the so-called war on terror. The world stood on the brink of a religious war to rival that of the crusades, and has yet to pull back completely from the precipice. The link between religious affiliation and political affiliation has consequently been strengthened to the extent that the particular religious status or beliefs of political leaders are now deemed newsworthy by the national press. Most religious press is not positive, however. Stories of fundamentalism, extremism, cults and sects vie for attention with stories of how homophobic or paedophilic the Church is. The good news is seldom news. Martin Luther King, Jr, is reputed to have said, 'The question is not whether we will be extremists, but what kind of extremists we will be . . . The nation and the world are in dire need of creative extremists.'

The vision that the wider world has of the Church bears little resemblance to the gospel, which is undoubtedly one of the key reasons why church attendance is declining. Without a concerted campaign to address the miscommunication of the gospel, this situation is unlikely to alter. One of the most important tasks in a pioneer ministry therefore is to communicate the good news as good news in its own right, rather than as an adjunct to some statement of denominational doctrine, or ecclesiology. The mantra should be, 'If you can't explain it simply, you don't understand it well enough.'

The vision that the pioneer has to share is of a community of disciples, intent on changing the world through loving service, one person at a time.

> Enthusing an on-going dialogue or relationship between Christian faith and local culture leads both at the conscious level, and at an unconscious level, to a reframing of the good news in a way that speaks to the local community.[9]

It is important however to hold on to the fact that the good news is proclaimed and communicated as much by the method we use to communicate it, as by what is actually said. Many people complain that the Church is anachronistic, that it needs a good marketing manager, but the Church has nothing to sell, God's grace is not the Church's to control and the worship or service of the Church is only a part of the work of the kingdom as long as it remains free. The Church nonetheless has to live in what is now a buyers' market. People are so accustomed to marketing and advertising that they are suspicious of anything that does not come with a suitably designed web page and internet presence. This has strengthened the 'what-have-you-done-for-me-lately' attitude that forms the basis of all too many pastoral relationships in the Church. There is more than a small grain of truth however to the idea that church people now have a consumeristic attitude to mission because we have trained them to think this way. When churches buy their mission packs from the shelf, proudly hang up the ready made banners outside the buildings and 'sell' the branded worship to the largest crowd possible, they simply reinforce a consumer mind-set that sits very uncomfortably with a gospel of free – albeit costly – grace. Branded worship attempts to cater to the demands of the secular world by repackaging the gospel so that it will appeal to targeted sections of the population.

> Our church lives in a buyer's market where the customer is king. What the customer wants the customer should get. With half a notion of the gospel, pastors who get caught up in this web of buying and selling in a self-fulfilment economy will one day wake up and hate themselves for it.[10]

The gospel's appeal is that it stresses that God doesn't see people in the same way that the world does. Being transformed by the gospel does not mean being changed into a middle-class, squeaky-clean suburbanite. The aim of the gospel is not to make people respectable in the eyes of society; it is to make them reconciled to God.

Advertising and marketing can have good short-term results. This can be very helpful in attracting people to an event, a launch or a service of some kind. But they are generally part of the 'come-to-us' approach to mission and church. The most effective way to communicate a fresh expression of church is by word of mouth, in and about the local community. This may not attract the same crowds, but pioneering isn't about crowds, it is about community. Those who have been helped by the service already offered as part of the ministry will want tell others; the gospel is gossiped when those who share it have something good to gossip about. The small miracles of service that make life bearable, enjoyable, fun and fulfilling are good news. When people's lives are changed by a cup of tea, a handshake, a hot meal, a clean needle, a clean street, or just a helping hand, they tend to tell others about it. Scripture records repeatedly how even though Jesus told people not to tell anyone about the transformation he had wrought in their lives, the response was always the same – news of Jesus spread throughout the region. Good ministry is noised abroad when it communicates the work of God.

Expect success

It can be disconcerting to discover how few of those who are trying to pioneer a community centred on a transformational belief in God have sufficient belief in their own calling or in God to expect the venture to succeed.

Most pioneering ventures or fresh expressions are hedged around with the language of cautious optimism, uncertainty and calculated risk, presumably so that if they do not achieve their desired outcomes, it will be less difficult for all involved to bear. Pioneers are accordingly primed to encounter problems, rather than prepared to expect all things to be made possible. This is completely contrary to the advice of Scripture. Jesus prepared his disciples for his departure by warning them in advance to expect success in their part in God's mission.

> Very truly, I tell you, the one who believes in me will also do the works that I do and, in fact, will do greater works than these, because I am going to the Father. I will do whatever you ask in my name, so that the Father may be glorified in the Son. If in my name you ask me for anything, I will do it. (John 14.12–14)

The very idea of the disciples doing greater works than Jesus was and is amazing, but it is also the pioneer's mandate to mission with every expectation of success.

Success has a different feel in pioneer ministry. It can't be measured as easily in terms of financial gain or numerical growth. A successful ministry is measured by the quality of the relationships that are formed between God and those being ministered to; the number of them is unimportant. It is measured in small but essential miracles, the miracle of people wanting to serve their community, the miracle of people wanting to live, the miracle of people actually knowing that the best of all is, God *is* with us.

Barack Obama won a presidential campaign in the USA based on the fact that the world wants to believe in the possibility of success, not in the certainty of failure. It is possible for the world to change, it is possible for lives to be transformed, it is possible for an army of ordinary people to work together and make a dream come true. 'Yes we can' is not just one man's political slogan, however, it is the Bible's promise to all God's people.

> Ask, and it will be given to you; search, and you will find; knock, and the door will be opened for you. For everyone who asks receives, and everyone who searches finds, and for everyone who knocks, the door will be opened. (Matt. 7.7–8)

Pioneer ministry can be seen as just one of the ways that the Church is asking for God to give it new life, to help it to find those who have been lost to it, and to open its doors to new, alternative Christian communities of faith. It is true that not everyone in the Church either understands or even agrees with fresh expressions of church, but all Christians recognize the call to mission and prayer for the Church of the future. Pioneers should expect this prayer of the Church to be answered, and for their ministry to succeed, not because of who they are, but because of who God is, and because God is not a liar.

> Again, truly I tell you, if two of you agree on earth about anything you ask, it will be done for you by my Father in heaven. For where two or three are gathered in my name, I am there among them. (Matt. 18.19–20)

The '10:2B virus', for example, started in Denver, Colorado, as a prayer movement of pioneers and church planters based on the words of Luke 10.2:

He said to them, 'The harvest is plentiful, but the labourers are few; therefore ask the Lord of the harvest to send out labourers into his harvest.'

Neil Cole narrates how 'catching' this virus and actually asking God made a significant difference to the success of Organic Church.

> Every morning at 10:02 A.M. my electronic organizer is programmed to have an alarm go off and remind me to beg God for more labourers. I started praying the 10:2B prayer in December 2003. At that time our association had only 42 church planters. By late January 2004 we had more than eighty.[11]

The call to participate in the *Missio Dei* is a call to succeed in enabling a particular part of God's mission to happen according to God's plan.

4

Maturing

One of the definitions of a fresh expression states:

> It will have the potential to become a mature expression of church shaped by the gospel and the enduring marks of the church and for its cultural context.[1]

Although this seems to be quite a specific definition, it is in fact very ambiguous as there is no consensus as to what a 'mature expression of church' actually looks like, particularly one intended for a specific cultural context. According to the Anglican Diocese of Norwich, 'these mature expressions of church need not look like traditional expressions of church'.[2] In Newcastle it is believed that 'these fresh expressions of church and community mission initiatives are as diverse as the different contexts of the Diocese of Newcastle'.[3]

In answer to the question, 'When does a fresh expression of church become a mature community?' Steve Croft[4] refers explicitly to Article 19, which states,

> The visible Church of Christ is a congregation of faithful men and women, in which the pure Word of God is preached, and the Sacraments be duly administered according to Christ's ordinance in all those things that of necessity are requisite to the same.[5]

He believes that as new forms of church mature, questions relating to the ordering of ministry, deciding who can preach, what shapes worship and how the sacraments are to be administered will need to be addressed. These questions of ecclesiology are important and cannot be ignored as long as mission is concerned with the growth of the Church.

As has already been covered in Chapter 1, an authentic fresh expression of church will undoubtedly possess all the 'enduring marks of the Church'. It will be one, holy, catholic and apostolic. What is less certain is that it must or necessarily will 'mature' in such a way that it becomes a part of the visible Church of Christ as defined by Article 19a of the Anglican articles of institution. As fresh expressions of church and pioneer ministries are making all too evident, the Church is much more than the place where the Word of God is preached, and the sacraments are duly administered in the same way that they have been for the last few hundred years.

Inherited church preaching tends to presume a priority and an emphasis on the spoken word that is out of keeping with the increasing trend towards visual and multi-sensory forms of communication. Similarly, the current rubrics in the traditional Church for administering the sacraments largely presume that the community will physically gather to share together, something that is not possible or not expected of many network churches and virtual faith communities.

The confidence needed to grow or mature a fresh expression of church is unlikely to come from the imposition of traditional or inherited ecclesiology – regardless of how sensitive or well intentioned. The confidence and ability will only come from holding to the original motivation to grow the kingdom of God through making disciples of Jesus Christ:

> Go therefore and make disciples of all nations, baptizing them in the name of the Father and of the Son and of the Holy Spirit, and teaching them to obey everything that I have commanded you. And remember, I am with you always, to the end of the age.
>
> (Matt. 28.19–20)

It is worth noting that Jesus did not command the disciples to go and make churchgoers of all nations. This is not meant to imply that ecclesiology is unimportant; it is very important, but it is not the pioneer's task to transform community into church. Growth in pioneering should never be confused with growth in churchmanship.

How then should the pioneer expect to grow a fresh expression of church which is succeeding as expected? The answer lies in continuing the preparation that preceded the ministry. Following on from the discourse in John's Gospel in which Jesus startles the disciples by telling them that they will do greater works than he has done, Jesus tells them how. He says:

> Those who love me will keep my word, and my Father will love them, and we will come to them and make our home with them.
>
> (John 14.23)

Pioneer ministry grows and matures when it remains rooted in the two great commandments, especially in the love of God. Growing, maturing or perfecting a fresh expression of church is as dependent on the grace of God as planning, preparing and initiating it is. The pioneer has to remain open to being a responsible participant in the work of God. To this end pioneers should look to respond still further to God's grace and:

- Grow the ministry
- Reflect and respond
- Adapt
- Challenge
- Enable and exit.

Grow the ministry

The surest way to end a pioneering ministry is to attempt to grow the expression of it rather than the ministry. As soon as pioneers slip into the 'come to church' mentality, even if it is an invitation to 'come to the fresh expression of church', they will have lost the pioneering edge that enabled them to reach out. As someone once said, 'Our current systems are perfectly designed to produce the results we are now seeing.' Trying to grow a pioneer ministry using the same methodologies as those used in traditional church planting or expansion will simply reproduce the same culturally insensitive contexts that pioneer ministry is called to bypass. Growing a fresh expression entails growing the ministry that initiated it, rather than the visible expression of it. Christianity did not grow by gathering together everyone who knew of or had heard of Jesus, or even by reproducing what was happening at Jerusalem in Antioch, or elsewhere. It grew when the number of people who could share in the pioneering task multiplied and took the ministry they had received and adapted it for their specific contexts.

Ministry grows by reproduction not by addition. According to Bob Logan, a leading church strategist,

> The best way to reach the harvest isn't through large churches, or even through planting more churches, but through churches that multiply – whatever their size. What we need is a Church Multiplication Movement![6]

One of the reasons that this is so important in pioneer ministry is that fresh expressions of church are not concerned with trying to increase the size of congregations but with building Christian communities through service and Christian fellowship.

A community that is forced to grow past its natural size quickly becomes dis-eased and unable to function as it should. It is for this reason that although many churches would be thrilled by the sort of numerical growth that Jacob's Well has experienced (1,000 attenders after seven years of existence), its founder, Tim Keel, worries that this growth may mean that it is no longer intimate enough to nurture community and friendship. The ministry matters more to him than numerical or even financial growth. In a sermon on church stewardship he insisted that the church didn't need any more money or volunteers, so giving of time or money should come only out of genuine gratitude.[7]

Once a community reaches its natural size, it will either reproduce itself, or stay at the same level for a while and then die away; this is what natural healthy living things do.

> We're not looking for fresh expressions to go on and on and on and on. We're expecting an organic life cycle for them. And we're expecting that as part of that life cycle that some will multiply, some will die, some will be passed on to new leaders who will bring new vision to it and take it into a new phase of its life.[8]

Reflect

Neglecting the health and inner life of missional communities undermines the confidence of those who are sharing faith with their friends, disenchants any who begin to belong before they believe and accelerates the exodus of believers. Building healthy honest and harmonious communities is a prerequisite for effective mission.[9]

Ministry that is pioneering and experimental sometimes inadvertently shifts from being the means to being the message. Part of the oversight of a growing ministry should be regular reflection on key questions such as:

- Where is God in this?
- Am I happy with and fulfilled in this ministry?
- Who does this ministry serve?
- How does this ministry enable Christ to be present/recognized/ celebrated?
- In what way does this ministry bring glory to God?
- Who or what is being 'advertised' in the ministry?
- Whose name is most up-front and visible and why?
- What makes this a distinctively Christian ministry?

There are no right or wrong answers as each person's ministry is different. What matters is taking the time regularly to reflect. It is this that will enable the pioneer to not lose sight of the two commandments.

One of the easiest ways of learning to reflect is to keep a journal. A journal is more than a diary of events; it is the record of an active conversation with God. Journalling or blogging the work of the ministry provides the pioneer with a spiritual record of thoughts and prayers concerning the work. Reread weeks later, it can provide highly pertinent information to assist in the pioneer's reflections on the above questions.

Another way to reflect is to do as St Paul and the Gospel writers did, write letters to the communities that you are forming and to those that are working with you in the ministry. What problems are the community facing, what advice would you offer based on your love of God and their knowledge of the gospel? The letters need never be sent, but writing them aids in the reflective process, enabling the pioneer to see the links between the growth of the community, the love of God and the work that is being done. St Paul's example and advice is worth following:

Finally, beloved, whatever is true, whatever is honourable, whatever is just, whatever is pure, whatever is pleasing, whatever is commendable, if there is any excellence and if there is anything worthy of praise, think about these things.   (Phil. 4.8)

Adapt

In the last quarter of a century, the computer and modern telecommunications have revolutionized the way in which a significant proportion of society now chooses to communicate, to shop, to socialize, read and research. While most churches are still only fiddling and fussing over PowerPoint and digital projectors, the world moves on to Second-Life services, podcasts and Twittering. High-speed telecommunications have changed so much more than the manner in which people communicate, they have effectively redefined huge sections of community. It is no longer either necessary, or desirable in some instances, for people to 'live together in unity'. It is easy enough to MSN, Skype or webcam across the globe, telecommute to work and 'meet' and even date online.

Changes in social cohesion over a similar time period have also been marked. Although the number of people moving home in the UK seems to be declining, the number of households has actually increased by almost a third and is projected to grow still further. The family unit is now smaller than it has been at any time. The number of children living in lone-parent families has more than tripled so that they now account for almost a quarter of all children in the UK.[10] The global village is a reality with about one person in every 15 in the UK coming from an ethnic minority group.

While some of these changes are visible in the composition of local church congregations, it is also evident that, on the whole, the Church is struggling to keep up with the rapid pace of social change. As Murray points out, in the 1980s many asked how churches could grow, in the 1990s many asked how churches could multiply, in the 2000s some are asking how churches can survive.[11] The pioneer on the other hand is uniquely placed to continue to minister to these changing contexts because he or she is immersed in them.

A growing pioneering ministry will be a barometer of social change, continually adapting to the new context in which it finds itself. 'The King's Crown' is a good example. This small pioneering ministry started as a Christian discussion group in a pub and called itself CAMRA (Christ and Me – the Real Alternative) as a deliberate play on the name of the Campaign for Real Ale. When, two years after its formation, the pub was bought out by a major brewery house, the group reformed itself as 'The King's Crown' – again, a play on the name, this time of the pub which had been changed to The Rose and Crown. Although only a change of name, it was significant enough to attract the attention of a few other 'locals'. The group's loyalty to both Christ and the pub was rewarded by an invitation from the manager to host a regular small act of worship once a month and to lead a carol service at Christmas. What adapting congregations seem to do well is to create opportunities for different constituencies to meet, and in particular to eat together.

Pioneers know that we are all part of this world and are inextricably bound up in its culture. They are therefore looking to continuously adapt their ministries in response to change, so that they not only meet the needs that the changes throw up, but are able to seize the opportunities for new ministry that they provide. As Tim Keel says of Jacob's Well, 'We can't assume that because God has blessed what we've done in the past here at Jacob's Well that he will again. We serve a living God, and are hardly the same as we were a year or two ago.'[12]

Challenge

The work of Jesus was not a new set of ideals or principles for reforming or even revolutionizing society, but the establishment of a new community, a people that embodied forgiveness, sharing and self-sacrificing love in its rituals and discipline. In that sense, the visible church is not to be the bearer of Christ's message, but to be the message.[13]

The challenge of being the message of the gospel is attractive and compelling, and the easiest way to grow a fresh expression of church is to share that challenge. All too often, especially in the early days of a ministry, pioneers are too hesitant to share the challenge, often out of what they consider to be genuine pastoral care for others. All that this succeeds in doing however is disenfranchising those whom God may be calling to participate. Just as the pioneers would not want to be spared the mixed blessing of the challenge and risk of the ministry they have been called to, so it is inappropriate for them to deny it to others. Scripture records how the disciples strengthened and encouraged each other in times of adversity saying:

> 'It is through many persecutions that we must enter the kingdom of God.' And after they had appointed elders for them in each church, with prayer and fasting they entrusted them to the Lord in whom they had come to believe. (Acts 14.22–23)

Research into ways of motivating has repeatedly shown that if people are presented with a realistic but challenging goal they are more likely to strive for it than if they are presented with something within their capability. According to one of the most popular books on motivation:

> only challenge causes growth. Only challenge will test our skills and make us better. Only challenge and the self motivation to engage in the challenge will transform us. Every challenge we face is an opportunity to create a more skillful self.[14]

Humanity is called to be more than it currently is, it is called to be renewed and transformed into the image of the living God. This, it would seem, is encoded in the human psyche to such an extent that it is almost instinctive to want to rise to a challenge. 'Groups will atrophy if you don't have a system for giving them challenge and a vision to multiply.'[15]

When Jesus called his disciples to take up their crosses and follow him, he was inviting them to accept the challenge of being the message, of living so like him that they might end up sharing the same fate as him, yet the disciples were not deterred by this.

Belonging to a fresh expression of church should be a call to discipleship so challenging that those who take up the challenge will be consumed by it. It is a lifelong challenge that affects every aspect of life, not just one hour on a Sunday. Growing a pioneering ministry is about communicating the positives of this challenge so that those who hear it will be demanding the right to invest in it.

Neil Cole offers the following biting critique of normal church life.

> We ask for volunteers all the time. We offer spiritual-gift assessments to see where people fit best in our program, but we never really offer very challenging experiences for people. Handing out bulletins, directing traffic wearing a bright orange vest, chaperoning a youth function, or changing a diaper in the nursery may be helpful for the church program, but none of it is a task worth giving your life to. Many who struggle to do these things have a nagging unspoken question: 'Did Jesus come so I can do this?'[16]

The challenge is not to grow 250 members by a fixed date, or to double the attendance at a fixed expression within a given period of time, or even to become self-funding before the end of the contract. The challenge is simply – to be the message that Christ wants to proclaim to this community. When pioneers invite others in their community to share with them in that task, then the community begins to grow and be transformed into a kingdom community. When they assume that they alone are charged with that task, their ministry declines.

Enable and exit

Generating and maintaining the energy and enthusiasm necessary for a pioneering ministry is God's task. God is particularly good at this, but is often only invited to do so when the pioneer becomes desperate. What is so quickly forgotten is that the passion and enthusiasm that pioneers have for the ministry they feel called to is God's gift to them. God has enabled them to minister and God can and does enable others to provide the support necessary for the work to be done and to take over at the appropriate time. Scripture testifies to how effective the Spirit is at breaking through closed doors and minds: regardless of where potential pioneers and their supporters huddle together in locked rooms, God can and does break in to empower and energize them for mission and ministry. The story of Christ's ascension and of Pentecost is a recurrent story in Christian history.

Experience teaches, however, that it is much easier to put out a fire than to light one. It can often seem in pioneering ministry that there is far more interest in damping enthusiasm than in generating it. A common mistake that many pioneers make in response to this is to believe that they, and they alone, must somehow do everything necessary to continue to sustain the ministry that God has called them to initiate. There is nothing in Scripture to support this mistaken belief, although it is very contemporary to believe that God only helps those who help themselves. Pioneers who are inclined to believe that they are personally responsible for inspiring the full participation of others in the work of the ministry should perhaps reflect on the fact that there is nothing in Luke's account of Pentecost to suggest that the disciples only caught fire after they were given a rousing sermon by Peter: that came afterwards. Peter may have been called to build the Church and to preach the first post-ascension sermon, but the future of the Church was not in his hands alone, and he did not have to personally inspire the rest of the disciples or those whom God later called to share in mission such as Stephen, Saul, Barnabas, Timothy and Silas. That was the work of the Holy Spirit.

Recognizing God as the originating source of a pioneering ministry does not, however, absolve the pioneer from the responsibility to enable others to be able to take over the leadership and work of the ministry. Jesus began his ministry by training and preparing those who would be required to continue it after his ascension. This was not an accident, the disciples were key to the spread of the gospel throughout the world. It has been argued that churches only grow when the minister stays for a significant period of time. This may be true, but pioneer ministry is not interested in growth by addition but in growth by multiplication. The pioneer is called to initiate not sustain a ministry. The gifts that are needed to begin a project are seldom the same as those required to continue or maintain a project. This may not always be immediately apparent, as it is not always easy to identify when something moves out of the initiation phase. Often, continued growth is mistakenly interpreted as evidence that the project is still in the process of being built up. Again, the challenge to pioneers is to recognize when their specific gifts are being called upon. Pioneers are initiators, rather than pastors. Consider for example the difference between St Paul and James when the Church was still being formed. James was the head of the Church in Jerusalem. He did not leave it, but administered it. There is no record of him doing any missional outreach, only of him being the public face of what was being built. St Paul, on the other hand, did not stay in one place until that church was secure; he planted the seed, trained the leadership and moved on. He multiplied the work of God precisely by having the courage to move on to the next community. Paul entrusted the work that he started to God. It wasn't easy. His letters testify to the unease that he felt in doing this; the bond that is formed in ministry is deep and abiding. All ministers find it difficult to leave behind those that they have personally nurtured in the faith, it is however essential for faith to flourish.

In most churches when it is known that the minister is going to be absent, attendance actually drops, as though it is the minister that people have come to see, not Jesus. The often highly individualistic nature of contemporary pioneer ministry can make it difficult to let go of the very thing that it might seem has helped to draw the people into the presence of God. The more dependent a particular ministry is on the entrepreneurial and charismatic gifts of the pioneer, the harder it can be to keep it as a work of God. Courage and confidence in the purpose of the ministry and in the calling of the pioneer is needed to take time out and/or walk away as necessary, leaving what is precious in God's hands for as long as it takes.

To grow a fresh expression of church best, pioneers need to know how to leave it. They should plan, from the very start of any new venture, to look out for the God-sent future leaders of it and to resist the temptation to outstay their welcome and cripple the ministry of those God has called. It is hard to resist the temptation to judge who is and who is not crucial to the future growth of the ministry, but the one person who is not crucial is the pioneer who initiated it.

If Jesus could leave the future care of the Church in the hands of fishermen and tax collectors, then on what basis does a pioneer claim the need to stay once it is clear that the message has been heard?

> Now to him who by the power at work within us is able to accomplish abundantly far more than all we can ask or imagine, to him be glory in the church and in Christ Jesus to all generations, for ever and ever. Amen. (Eph. 3.20–21)

Part 2

CONGREGATIONS AND PIONEER MINISTRY

5

Mixed economy

Do you not say, 'Four months more, then comes the harvest'? But I tell you, look around you, and see how the fields are ripe for harvesting. The reaper is already receiving wages and is gathering fruit for eternal life, so that sower and reaper may rejoice together. For here the saying holds true, 'One sows and another reaps.' I sent you to reap that for which you did not labour. Others have laboured, and you have entered into their labour.

(John 4.35–38)

There are two reasons why fresh expressions of church are happening: either

- the gospel is being communicated so effectively that the existing church structures and systems cannot contain the growth of the kingdom; or
- the gospel is being communicated so badly that only by escaping existing church structures and systems can the kingdom continue to grow.

The truth, of course, is somewhere between the two. In some parts of the country, fresh expressions are happening naturally because of the ongoing commitment to local mission of existing local churches. In other places however they are happening primarily because people are so dissatisfied with their local church's inability or reluctance to engage in local mission that they attempt to address this lack themselves through forming a fresh expression of church. In either scenario, the local church played a key role, and must continue to do so for the sake of the unity and the future of the Church although in a more positive and constructive manner than has sometimes been the case in the past.

The communal and ecclesial question that is fundamental to the church's staying the church is what sort of community would we have to be in order to be the sort of people who live by our convictions?[1]

The Church cannot exist without pioneering ministry working alongside the more traditional forms of ministry. Scripture teaches that these two things belong together. They are not mutually exclusive or contradictory, but are equally valid and complementary means of participating in the *Missio Dei*. The unfortunate nomenclature of contemporary mission and ecclesiology, coupled with the extent to which the main denominations are investing time and money in pioneer ministry, has led understandably to a small degree of resentment or irritation from some churches and ministers. 'If', they ask, 'we are not leading a "fresh expression" of church as part of a "pioneering" ministry, are we deemed to be leading stale expressions of church or conducting a "stuck in the mud" ministry?' The answer is no, and the churches are seeking ways of demonstrating commitment to ecclesial diversity through the promotion of what has been called 'mixed economy'. Borrowing from the world of business, the Archbishop of Canterbury, Rowan Williams, referred to the practice of fresh expressions and inherited churches existing alongside each other as 'mixed economy'. The conviction is that only by working together in relationships of mutual respect and support can fresh and inherited expressions of church serve to build up the body of Christ and proclaim the good news effectively to today's highly pluralistic and fragmented society. Thus the online guide to fresh expressions declares that a commitment to the mixed economy of existing and new forms of church is one of the three characteristics of a fresh expression of church.

The gospel cannot be confined to human structures but will always outgrow, reshape and reform every attempt that is made to contain or tame it. The Church, as the body of Christ, like Christ, can have no place to lay its head. It is called to be continually moving towards the end of the age and its final consummation as part of the reconciliation of all creation. The history of the Church is the history of its movement in mission towards that goal. The Promised Land lies ever before the Church, which is called to follow where God leads it and to resist the temptation to put down roots. The Church may be called to rest sometimes, but never to halt its progress.

From the time of the first pioneer minister, Abraham, the people of God have been called to build – and then to move on – not least because when they do not, they tend to become so attached to their buildings that they lose sight of what is most important to them. The almost unprecedented opportunities for ministry now being recognized are a consequence of the Church having stayed too long in the same place, in spite of the fact that society has moved on.

Notwithstanding the growth of the house-church cell-church movement, the predominant understanding of what is meant by a 'local church' is still a stone building situated somewhere at the centre of a community. The reality however is often startlingly different. The likelihood of any church that was built more than fifty years ago still being at the geographical heart of the community it was originally designed to serve is now exceedingly small, as any survey of parish maps makes evident. Changes in society, in particular the fact that the population is now far more mobile than it ever has been in the past, coupled with the increase in population density following the 1960s, have encouraged the creation of new-towns and suburbs that to a large extent have ignored traditional parish boundaries. These 'new' communities tended to be built around train stations or shopping centres, or even industrial parks, rather than a village green or recreational park. In some places, this movement of the centre of the community has meant that the local parish church is peculiarly stranded on the outskirts of a modern town or suburb, a lonely reminder of the former village community that existed before the town planners did their work.

The full impact of this movement was often hidden by coincidental improvements in private and public transport. These made it possible for people to continue to attend their 'local' church even when, often for reasons of social mobility, they and their families had long since moved out of the immediate locality. When these two phenomena occurred together, as they invariably did, churches became increasingly isolated not only by virtue of their location, but by virtue of the fact that the worshipping congregation had little in common with the local residents of the surrounding areas. The human propensity for homogeneity meant that people moving into the new towns and suburbs were unlikely to be attracted to a church attended largely by those who had left the locality.

Working together

> We have to ask whether we are capable of moving towards a 'mixed economy' church, recognising church where it appears and having the willingness and the skill to work with it.[2]

Mixed economy grants the Church time to properly address the situation it finds itself in at the start of a new century. It makes it possible for those churches or circuits that do find themselves inadvertently culturally and/or physically isolated to continue to minister to the needs of their existing loyal congregation while still engaging in a fresh expression of church or pioneering a new ministry to the surrounding community for the sake of the future. It effectively grants existing churches the time to reposition themselves as necessary. In spite of earlier acquiescence to the human preference for homogeneous communities, therefore, mixed economy makes it possible for the Church to look boldly to the future and honour and promote the kingdom values of inclusivity and equality in diversity. It enables and encourages churches to seize the God-given opportunities for pioneer ministries and for fresh expressions of church without necessarily having to sacrifice everything it worked to achieve as a place of rest and recuperation for the soul.

There are significant advantages for both pioneers and pastoral ministers to work together out of the same church. For the pioneers, the church provides first and foremost the means of grace that will keep them rooted in their faith and enable them to grow in grace and holiness as they undertake their ministry. The church is also usually able to share in the oversight of the developing ministry; it can offer assistance through prayer support as well as providing practical support in terms of financial assistance, the loan of equipment, a space to work, collegiality, and opportunities to learn and train.

From the church's point of view, pioneers effectively create time and space for the church to explore its own calling and to consider the wider mission and ministry opportunities afforded by its (often not inconsiderable) capital assets and human resources. Pioneers' enthusiasm for mission and for the proclamation of the gospel is usually quite infectious and can be used by the wider church to motivate vision and leadership throughout the congregation. Their often uncomplicated, seemingly unorthodox views on the work of the church, on the conduct of worship and on the structure of Christian community and the meaning of discipleship for the twenty-first century could afford an entire congregation a glimpse of the potential for God's work among the unchurched of their community. Pioneers can offer an existing church hope for the future by their choice to remain linked to the traditions of the past and by their willingness to teach others how to share them and speak of them in the language and idiom of the present. Above all, pioneers help to form a cultural bridge for an existing church to cross what otherwise might seem like an impossible chasm. They do this by encouraging and inspiring the church to let go of its preconceptions and become attuned to and understand the social and spiritual realities of the people outside rather than inside the church.

> The New Place in the inner city of Bristol was also directly underneath the M32, it was a community living under and often divided by the shadow of a huge concrete motorway in the sky, of underpasses streaked with graffiti and strewn with used needles. We set about looking at our environment and setting up mini altars, places where heaven may be found, this developed from the outside environment into people's homes, to children's activities, to a multitude of places and people where we felt we touched with God, where heaven existed.[3]

The Church has the same opportunity as every other service provider in this postmodern world. It may be called to be both a physical presence in a local community and a hub that serves a wider dispersed community through a deliberately constructed network (which may, or may not, make use of information technology to sustain it). It may be called solely to serve a section of the local community or even a sub-section of a virtual community. The knowledge that these options exist can be wonderfully liberating for a church. It can release an existing congregation to think more creatively about almost every aspect of the church's visible physical presence, from its building through to the staff it employs.

Knowing that it has choices it can make often empowers a congregation to dare ask whether it needs its existing church buildings, or whether somewhere else might be more appropriate to the specific ministerial as opposed to geographical context in which the church is located. Similarly, having a clearer understanding of the nature of its context can stimulate a church to think creatively, to reflect and discern the level of staff needed to release the full potential of the church and congregation for ministry. What a church dare not do, given the changes that have taken place in society and the way in which relationships and communities are formed and maintained, is assume that it can just continue as it is. Every church needs regularly to consider whether it is still called to serve the same community that it was originally created to serve, and whether it is still known by the people of that community.

The Church cannot afford to underestimate the significance of the emergence of pioneer ministers, and fresh expressions of church. As was pointed out at the start of this chapter, pioneer ministry is as much a statement of the Church's failure to communicate the gospel in ways that are contemporary and relevant as it is of its determination to make the attempt to do so. It would accordingly be a serious mistake to trust the future of the Church to a belief in a lingering notional Christianity that can somehow be fanned into flames again if the right decisions are taken by Conference or by the General Synod. The reality is that the Church can no longer assume that the community it is called to serve has any significant knowledge of the Christian faith, or any desire to know about God. The social structures that once underpinned regular Sunday church attendance have rightly been altered to take account of religious plurality and promote racial equality. Although the working week is still divided into work days and rest days, Sunday is no longer reserved as a societal 'day of rest'. Sporting and social events are just as likely to take place on a Sunday as they are on a Saturday. In order to earn a place of love and respect in the life of a local community, therefore, the church will need to ensure that something intrinsic in its worship, outreach and ministry serves the needs of the community and is of real interest to them. Sunday is no longer the first day in the week for most people, and the church is no longer at the centre of every village or community. If the church wants to continue to live a vibrant life of service to God and to neighbour, then it will have to relearn how to be an active participant and shaper of this wonderfully multi-dimensional world.

Mapping the potential

Pioneer ministers operate under the assumption that this is an age when Christianity is increasingly seen as just one more possible consumer choice for a once-a-week leisure-time activity rather than a life-determining decision. They know that most people are biblically illiterate and totally uninformed about the good news of Jesus Christ. They believe that a significant proportion of the Church's practices, worship, systems and structures can seem completely irrelevant to most people's everyday lives and a real hindrance to the proclamation of the gospel so that it can be heard and responded to.

The good news is that the Church has been here before and, by the grace of God, is still here. By listening to and responding to the will of God for God's people, the Church has learned how to adapt its structures, rebuild and refocus its ministry where appropriate, and proclaim the gospel such that it can be heard and responded to. What it has done before, it can, if God so wills it, do again. The increasing number of young people offering for lay and ordained pioneer ministry across the denominations can be read as a sign of God's determination to reshape and equip the Church for the challenges of this age. They can also be seen as an invitation for the rest of the Church to join in, to consider what might need preserving and what might need changing in response to the needs of this age. The initial response of many churches is to try and change the style of worship for a Sunday or a weekday service. They often do this without engaging in any research into the community or the people that they are hoping this new worship will attract. Such changes in worship are effectively made because the church wants to make them, or believes them to be necessary. What needs to happen is for the church to love the community enough to find out what they want or need.

This means being willing to ask fundamental questions about the nature and purpose of the local church, why it is where it is, and how, if at all, it should change its purpose, worship and nature in response to the challenges of the times. This can be greatly assisted by studying the society that the church is part of and is called to minister to. As John Patton has observed, 'the social situation in all its uniqueness should inform the thought and action of the reflection of the Christian community'.[4] Thankfully there are tools to help a church investigate these questions and discern their answers based on faith and fact.

It has always been important for people to know how things are arranged spatially and how they might have to change with time, whether they are primitive hunters deciding how best to stalk their next meal or twenty-first-century pioneer ministers trying to determine where the Church of the future might be. The increasing mobility of the population and astonishing speed of contemporary industrialization has made it more important than ever for information about spatial relationships and sociopolitical and religious trends to be collected and analysed as a natural part of the Church's self-awareness and discernment of its calling. It might not seem very spiritual, but it is very scriptural. How can the Church reach out in ministry and be, as Paul seemed to imply that it must, metaphorically speaking, as a Greek to the Greeks, or as a Jew to the Jews, when it does not know enough about its community to know whether there are any Greeks or how or where to find a Jew? The fact is that communities are no longer limited to geographically defined associations.

The Church's role is 'to influence change by walking alongside her neighbours and in particular by each congregation being in partnership with its local community'.[5] To do this effectively, the local church has to know the community. While it may once have been the case that most people were born and raised in the same general locality where they also lived, worked, worshipped and raised their own families before retiring and finally being laid to rest, the same is not generally the case today. People are far more socially and geographically mobile. Developments in information technology have also encouraged the creation of communities that can span the globe. It is now possible to initiate and sustain close friendships and working relationships across several different continents via emails and text messages, social networks, websites and weblogs. These networked communities are just as real to those who are part of them, as the village community once was in the countryside a few hundred years ago. An increasingly large number of people 'meet' their partners on the internet, and some claim that they grew to love each other in cyberspace long before they eventually met up in 'real' space.

Demographic, socio-political and geospatial information can assist a church in understanding its place in a community, whatever sort of community that might be. This data is an extension of the statistical data that the church should have already been collecting on a regular basis concerning its own membership. Given the link that statistical returns often have with finances, however, this data is often the most inaccurate or misleading. In the end, this is more harmful than helpful to the future viability of a church. As Nigel McCulloch has noted, 'God's mission is more likely to be furthered if the Church has an accurate picture and honest appraisal of its numbers – and uses that information to enable it to find fresh ways of communicating the ageless Gospel message.'[6]

When it is accurate and reliable, statistical information can help to reveal the needs and aspirations of specific communities as well as the way in which those needs have changed over time. It can highlight areas of growth and of decline, and even offer reasoned predictions and trends on subjects as diverse as crime or divorce rates, future educational needs, and even church attendance. This information is available to the church to assist it to discern how God may be calling it to serve a specific community. In these increasingly uncertain times, it can afford a valuable insight into what type of community a church is best placed to serve: local or typical. Is the community formed predominantly by its *geographical* location, or is it formed by a *type* – of person or worship or theology, or whatever? These two community models are not the same.

A community formed by location is related in a meaningful and specific way to a particular place. A local church congregation whose membership is drawn almost exclusively from that locality is a good example of this sort of community. A community formed by a particular category or type of person or worship style etc. is a community bound together by some common activity, or vocation, or by a shared interest or way of being such as young people, Christian counsellors or members of the Methodist Sacramental Fellowship. While the defining commonality may also imply that members are drawn from the same geographical area, this need not be the case. In most instances churches will discover that they are already serving many communities within a particular locality, local businesswomen, for example, or men's Bible fellowships. In some instances, the diversity of community served by the church has been a blessing both to the worshipping fellowship and to members of the locality. In others, the extent of the diversity, the sheer number of competing claims on its time and resources, has led to a real depletion of energy in congregations and a general confusion over what the role of the church actually is. Does the church exist to provide suitable premises for local community needs, or is it called to serve a more specific purpose?

Knowing what sort of community and what degree of multiplicity it is called to serve will impact on the sort of information that a church needs to collect and analyse and where it should go to look for it. While a church is still discerning its mission, however, it does no harm to collect both sets of data, local and typical.

Obtaining the necessary information is not difficult as in most countries it is freely available on the internet. In the UK for example, the national statistics office provides a free online service, which can easily be interrogated for detailed statistics.[7] Summary information for individual localities is provided at national level according to an area's postcode. More detailed local information is available sometimes through local government websites. Many national church bodies offer statistical information concerning their church attendance, sacramental and worship practices, denominational affiliations, and so forth either online or in printed format, all of which can add depth and colour to the purely factual information given in government statistics.

Geographic Information Systems (GIS) are software packages that combine maps and statistics with powerful imaging software to provide a more visual display of this sort of statistical information. They enable those who analyse the information they provide to recognize patterns of behaviour, social trends and even key issues and hence explore possible mission or service-oriented responses. They are increasingly used by a wide range of organizations, including government and private companies. Thanks to an innovative partnership initiative involving the National Church Institutions and the English dioceses, every diocese of the Church of England now has its own GIS. They are being used to provide many churches with the information necessary to rethink their

- pastoral reorganization
- land, property and asset management
- statistical analysis.

In Manchester, for example, it has already been recognized that GIS 'can be a tool for mission planning both by local parishes and the whole diocese'. It is used to explore the fine detail of parishes and local neighbourhoods. The examples cited include:

- provision of socio-demographic data to support parish and community audits;

- identification of particular areas and issues to support funding applications by parishes and community groups;
- impact studies to demonstrate the success of local church and community projects within the neighbourhood;
- mapping church buildings and schools within particular regeneration areas.

Manchester Diocese use their system to collate a parish information pack, which is then provided free of charge to parishes and people training for ministry on accredited courses. At the moment, the pack they compile for their churches contains:

- a colour A3 topographic map showing the parish boundary against a 1:10000-scale map;
- a colour A4 thematic map showing the parish boundary against the Index of Multiple Deprivation 2004;
- a report including select church data and statistics from the 2001 Census;
- a report listing the parish scores based on the Indices of Deprivation 2004;
- explanatory guides to the parish data.

Other dioceses and districts could provide similar data. It is not too difficult however to obtain it directly from a combination of local government sites, national church statistics and local libraries.

The basic information needed by every church can be summarized as follows:

- Who are the members of this community?
  - What is the age profile?
  - What is the racial profile?
  - What is the social profile?
  - What is the religious profile?
- What changes have there been over the last ten years?
  - How has the population changed?
  - How has the deprivation index changed?
  - How has the racial profile changed?
  - How has the religious profile changed?

- What is predicted to change over the next ten years?
  - What is the estimated population growth?
  - What major plans exist for economic growth?
  - What major building/social cohesion projects are planned?

The same sort of basic questions can be asked of both local and typical communities. Thus, for example, if a church decided that its primary community was Eastern European asylum seekers then it would be helpful for the church to build a full geographic profile from government census information so that it knew where the largest percentage of this community were living, outside of its own specific locality. This would enable the church to make informed decisions about who it might be able to work in partnership with, where existing help might be found, what transport, if any, would be needed, and so on.

The challenge is not in obtaining the data, but in interrogating and interpreting the data that has been obtained so that it serves the discernment processes and ministry objectives of the church. Although it is possible to hire the services of a specialist in this field, such services are usually quite expensive and often counterproductive. One of the most important benefits from undertaking the task as a church is the way in which the whole congregation can share in the interrogation and analysis process. There is always more than one way of reading statistical information. This is particularly true of data being collected to discern the potential for mission. What one person might interpret as a hindrance to the planned activity of the church, another might see as a challenging pioneering opportunity.

GIS and demographic data can provide information on a population's age, gender, marital status, education, income, attitudes, behaviour, race, ethnicity, and location. Analysed carefully this can then be used to explore answers to highly specific questions such as:

1 What are the age, race and gender of typical people from this community?
2 What do they do for a living?
3 What is their average income?
4 Are they more likely to be married or single?

5 What is the average size of the family they live with?
6 Do they have children, and if so, of what age?
7 What is their religion?
8 Do they attend worship?
9 What sort of a house do they live in, rented or owned?
10 What other significant population groups are a part of this community?
11 How many churches already exist in this area?
12 What is church attendance like in this area?
13 What other community facilities exist in this area?
14 What are the most common felt-needs in this community?

The temptation is always to attempt to study too much data at any one time. It is best to explore the possible answers to each of the specific questions in turn rather than trying to compile a complete picture immediately. Wherever possible it is also advisable to make use of one of the most helpful forms of data that there is – namely comparative data. This can be exceptionally helpful in predicting trends and uncovering what is either unique or commonplace about a particular aspect of a community. Doing multiple smaller studies of adjacent postcodes or age groups, for example, often yields far more useful information for comparative purposes than one or two larger studies would and tends to be much more helpful in narrowing the focus of potential forms of pioneering ministry or fresh expressions of church.

Regardless of how many smaller studies are done, it is almost always useful to be able to compare local or neighbourhood statistics with the larger regional or national statistics. If it knows, for example, that the proportion of families with below average income in one locality is significantly higher than the national average, then a church may be better able to bid for financial assistance from various philanthropic as well as civic bodies for its mission work. A significant number of national and international aid agencies will expect those seeking financial assistance to have undertaken the sort of statistical mapping outlined here.

Statistics can help a church to make more confident predictions about how receptive people in their area are likely to be to particular forms of ministry or expressions of church. If the statistical data shows that a typical person from the community, for example, is aged 63, widowed and living alone in her own accommodation, then starting a youth church might not be the best use of the church's money. On the other hand, if the statistics also show that the most significant shift in the population has been in the size of the immigrant community, which has as a typical member someone with an average age of 32, married with three children and living in rented accommodation, then a pioneer ministry to that smaller community now might prove to be a wise investment of resources for the future life of the church.

Churches with large buildings to maintain, and a limited budget, are not always able to respond as comprehensively as they might like to, to the needs of smaller community groups. The advantage of mixed economy is that they can, nonetheless, begin the process of change and of relocating the church to the centre of the community, spiritually and practically if not necessarily geographically, by supporting the work of a pioneer minister, or forming a small fresh expression of church specifically targeted to that group. Pioneers and fresh expressions of church then begin to function like fulcrum points or pivotal points for the ministry of the church. Without them, trying to move or turn something weighed down by over a century of history and tradition so that it can face the challenge of modern society would be almost impossible; the potential for friction alone would make most ministers turn away in horror. One pioneer, however, could begin the process, and in so doing alter the whole balance of energy needed to succeed and render the task manageable. More and more churches are finding that turning to face an uncertain future requires much less energy and effort with pioneers than without them.

A word of warning

'Figures often beguile me,' wrote Mark Twain, 'particularly when I have the arranging of them myself; in which case the remark attributed to Disraeli would often apply with justice and force: "There are three kinds of lies: lies, damned lies, and statistics."'

Every priest or minister who has ever had to make an annual return to the church is aware of how easy it is to massage figures to create a specific picture of a church community. One of the consequences of undertaking a study might be the realization that the church really is in the wrong place at the wrong time. Changing to match the needs of the surrounding community might be one step too far for a congregation. In such instances it might choose to close or seek other ways in which it might work in partnership with, for example, local charities or government agencies in order to fulfil its calling to serve God.

> No church wishing to remain faithful to the gospel can wish to conform to the world entirely; because of this it will inevitably be seen by society as standing apart. Partnership is therefore a better language than servanthood; the church serves the world but not because it is the world's servant.[8]

Alternatively, it is possible that the demographic data might be massaged to deceive a church body and to hide facts that are important but uncomfortable for mission. Census data can be summarized in such a way, for example, that the size of minority groups in a community can seem even smaller than they actually are. The financial information can similarly be downplayed such that it becomes possible to almost justify the neglect of nearby needy groups on the grounds of comparative wealth or something similar. Likewise, the data could be enhanced to make it appear as though there is a greater need than there actually is so as to argue in favour of a particular form of pioneering ministry or for the building or demolition of church premises or halls. Often the manipulation is not as a result of any deliberate attempt to deceive, but is due to a combination of a lack of skill in handling such data and over-enthusiasm of those seeking to use it constructively. There is, therefore, no real way of preventing this, but it is important to be alert to its possibility. The potential for such harm can be minimized by insisting on a regular review of local data, and by increasing the number of people engaged in the task of analysing it. Handled carefully with prayer, demographical and socio-political information can be a powerful aid in helping a church explore and release its pioneering potential for the sake of the future ministry of God to the whole community.

Ultimately, if we are honest, we need to acknowledge that there are no categories of 'them' and 'us' as if being men and women of faith somehow no longer makes us part of the human family. There is only the one valid category, 'we', humanity, the world, all of us together, one family inside a common search.[9]

6

Digging at the foundations

It is an essential condition of any traditional religious service that the space in which it is conducted must be invested with some measure of sacrality . . . if an audience is not immersed in an aura of mystery and symbolic otherworldliness, then it is unlikely that it can call forth the state of mind required for non-trivial religious experience.[1]

Valuing what exists

A popular children's nursery rhyme and hand game involves the words, 'here is the church, here is the steeple, open the doors and here are the people'. To many of those involved in the fresh expression movement, the idea of a fresh expression inside a church is an anathema. The last place you would find people, they claim, is inside the church. The Church is a turn-off – a hindrance to mission and to ministry rather than a Godsend or an asset. This may be the case, but it is not the church building that is being referred to in such statements; rather it is the hierarchy, the pomp and circumstance, the petty politics that are deemed irrelevant.

Recent research from Eastern Europe and from America suggests that far from being a millstone around the neck of a pioneer minister, a traditional built church can be the greatest asset that a minister has access to, and not because of the money that could be raised by selling or letting its space! The church has what many are crying out for – authentic sacred space, space that radiates the sort of prayerful peace that is the by-product of decades of regular worship and which is impossible to replicate or manufacture. This is one of the reasons that the Moot fresh expression of church,[2] which grew out of a desire to allow people to connect their daily, everyday lives with the sacred, using everyday technology, music, words and objects, likes to use a labyrinth[3] in some acts of worship. Gareth Powell says:

> One of the things that I think people are searching for today is authenticity. Using a very ancient form of liturgy allows people to connect to something that goes deeper than themselves and goes beyond themselves. And, in that way I think they see it as something authentic.[4]

The challenge facing the church that is serious about developing fresh expressions of church or releasing and equipping pioneer ministry is not how to rid itself of its property, but how to see its sacred space differently.

> Buildings introduce themselves by their sheer physical presence. Their size and scale, materials used, and sense of proportion and unity can draw our attention, bore us, or even repel us. Once past the initial 'introduction,' interesting buildings invite us to engage in a meaningful 'conversation,' holding out the promise of richer experiences embedded in their symbols and spaces.[5]

The Church needs to consider how its buildings could become the burning bush that draws people closer to question what they see, which makes them instinctively want to fall to their knees or remove their shoes; the place of refuge that keeps the flame of hope alive; the place of welcome, and of honest tears and prayers; the source of visions; and above all the place of encounter with God. It has to enable all those who seek, to find within it the permanence of faith, which can be tempered with the reminder that if necessary, this place too could be destroyed and raised again in three days, should God so will it. A tall order, but not impossible – and fresh expressions and pioneer ministry can really help. Because fresh expressions of church are working with those who are unchurched, they bring fresh eyes to gaze at what the gathered people of God can be, and what they have built. Sometimes what they see is critical, often they see what regular churchgoers no longer notice. The unchurched view church signs, symbols and space differently from those who do attend. Their preconceptions are drawn from a limited encounter with church, often as a result of what they have seen on TV or in the cinema, or read about in their newspapers. Children's nursery rhymes, Christmas nativities, harvest festivals, weddings, coronations and the weekly God-slot on TV create an illusion of church and what takes place in it, which is usually far from the reality of weekly worship. Their puzzlement at some of the practices of the church, at the robes and processions, the incense and the candles, can stimulate the church to reflect on the conduct of its worship, its inclusivity and openness to the honest enquirer, the warmth of its welcome and its accessibility to those not in the know.

Fresh expressions are in many ways an invitation to the church to consider whether or not it needs to revise some of its practices and the things that take place within the building. The building itself, however, is a well known and valued trademark of God which sometimes says more by its shape and structure about the work of God in the world than any advertising campaign ever could. The familiarity and yet distinctive 'otherness' of church buildings and their interiors can and does speak of a timeless truth which cannot be silenced or hidden away, regardless of how the world may change.

> The Church, as part of the city, has its own space. This is literally so in terms of buildings but is also symbolized in ritual and fellowship. It points to a different set of values; an alternative framework for viewing the world in the midst of the cares of daily existence. The celebration of the Eucharist is a political act, declaring that the creation has at its heart the fragility of sacrificial love.[6]

The process of discerning the mission of the church, which began with the acquisition and analysis of community data, continues with a full time-and-space audit of the church premises. Only once a church has a clear picture of what rooms are used when, by whom and what for, can it begin to ask of each room:

- When is this room used in service to the people of God?
- How does this room serve the mission of this church?
- In what way does the use of this room proclaim the presence of God to church people and to non-church people?

The most important question of the audit is the last one set for each room:

- How could this room be used differently as sacred space?

For an example of a full time-and-space audit for a room see the display panel below.

Time-and-space buildings audit – to be completed for each room

Room name

Dimensions (if possible please provide a rough scaled sketch)

Number of entrances and exits

Can the room be locked?

Is the room easily accessible for the disabled?

Is it possible to look into the room from outside with the doors shut?

How many windows does the room have?

Are the windows easy to open?

Are the windows protected?

Are the windows decorative?

Do the windows afford good light to the room?

Are there blinds or curtains for the windows to shield the room from light?

What permanent fixtures are in the room (e.g. pillars, stone altar, font or pulpit, raised dais, pews, etc.)?

What semi-permanent fixtures are in the room (e.g. removable communion rail, sound system, preaching lecterns, removable staging, etc.)?

What removable furniture (e.g. chairs, communion table, bookshelves, screens, etc.) is in the room?

What are the most attractive features of the room?

How well lit is the room?

How comfortable is the room in winter/summer?

What storage exists in the room? – Is it already used?

On what days is the room used, for what duration, and by whom?

What would need to be changed to transform this room into sacred space:
(a) In terms of its décor – does it need to be updated and redecorated?
(b) In terms of its furnishings – does old furniture need replacing?
(c) In terms of its general state of repair – are the floorboards worn or is the plaster falling off, etc.?
How could this room be used differently as sacred space?

This question and how it is answered reveals something fundamental about each church's perception of what constitutes sacred space and how it should be used. It is a sad reflection on the contemporary understanding of what it means to be church that although the sanctuary areas of the church may be in a fairly good state of repair, and designed to communicate a sense of the holy, often the ancillary rooms are not. Even in relatively new churches, there has been a tendency to create functional rather than inspirational rooms, as though God is only expected to be encountered in one part of the building. One reason, perhaps, why children are unlikely to think of church as attractive is that the rooms that they spend most time in when they are in church tend to be those least invested in, either aesthetically, financially or, more importantly, spiritually. The audit challenges the church to ask what there is in any of the 'function' rooms of the church that would remind those who use them that they are holy spaces, part of the house of God.

The difficulty facing long-standing church people is that they tend to have a fixed idea of what churches should be like, and in particular, what constitutes sacred space. Holy space is usually, but not always, associated with the liturgy, with the church's act of corporate worship. In practice, however, most rooms belonging to a church, whether in the church proper or ancillary rooms, could be, and arguably should be, sacred space, somewhere where people are enabled to encounter God.

All fresh expressions of church begin, as the work of the early Church did, with acts of service to the surrounding community. Through the service that practitioners offer in Christ's name, people are encouraged to become disciples, to be fellow servants who are willing to share in the work of the kingdom, whatever that might be. Only when the number of disciples warrants it, does a fresh expression tend to gather more formally and solely for worship. The first call on a church's building for a fresh expression of church, therefore, is most likely to be the ancillary rooms, the kitchens and the back rooms, where the community can meet and be fed, where children can be cared for, advice offered, facilities provided, and so forth.

Using the information gathered from the space-and-time audit, identify the strengths and weaknesses of each room as a sacred space – set aside by God for service. Think in terms of the room's space, shape, light, colour, decoration, sound quality, ambience, warmth, accessibility.

Next consider what, if anything, would need to be removed, changed or added to the room to make it attractive and suitable for: private prayer, public prayer, small group fellowship, sacramental worship, your daughter's wedding, your son's baptism, discussion, playtime, Bible-study, shared meals? Try not to think in terms of 'functionality' but in terms of attractiveness. What are the strengths of this room that would make people want to linger in it, relax in it and be able to be open and vulnerable in it? Similarly ask, what would inhibit people from using the space in these ways? It is worth doing this for three separate times of the day – morning, afternoon and evening, as rooms change character according to the amount of natural light they receive.

Most churches who undertake a time-and-space audit of their premises are surprised at what they discover about their church. Familiarity breeds contempt, and most church members stopped seeing the noticeboard many years ago. Few of the regular worshippers notice the faded picture of the blond-haired, blue-eyed Jesus standing in a garden with a lamp, or sitting in a forest clearing surrounded by small children and 'wild animals'. Similarly the picture of the past archbishop, or church founding father, on the vestry wall is no more noticed by the stewards or church-wardens than the fact that the covers are missing off some of the hymn books in the choir stalls. Trying to see church rooms as a visitor might is a challenging but worthwhile and very revealing exercise. Be prepared to find cupboards crammed with out-of-date papers, or broken toys from the last pre-school; old forgotten armchairs and tables languishing in corners; cracks in the paintwork, peeling plasterwork, worn steps, broken glass or windows that don't quite shut . . . yet this, all that the church has stopped noticing, is most often what a stranger notices first about God's house.

Most of the immediate concerns identified by an audit can usually be rectified quite easily and fall well within a church's normal maintenance budget. Cupboards can be cleaned and emptied, walls painted, floors re-sanded, glass replaced. Major concerns might need separate funding to be raised and permission to be obtained before they can be rectified, for example, new units to be fitted in the kitchen area or a disabled toilet to be installed. What can be done immediately, however, should be done so that the image of 'God's house' that a visitor receives is of a much-loved place of prayer.

Playing to strengths

God has been and continues to be at work in the Church. In spite of human frailty and often long-standing petty arguments about its internal décor or furniture, people have been able to encounter God in God's house. Contrary to popular opinion, it is not necessary to remove pews and pulpits, rip up organs or cover flagstones in order to make it fit for a fresh expression of church, any more than it is mandatory to have digital projections and a live band at every act of contemporary worship. As Ian Mobsby of Moot says,

> In a time where people are spiritually searching, actually there's something about liturgies that are quite transcendent and super spiritual that actually enable people to encounter something positive.[7]

What *is* important is that the use of sacred space and the worship that is offered by the church, fresh or inherited, matches the actual needs discerned by the community profile drawn up in the previous chapter. The church at worship continues to be the acid test for all parish ministries. In our worship, we retell and are held accountable to the story about what God is doing with us in Christ. All ministries can be evaluated by essentially liturgical criteria: How well does this act of ministry enable people to be with God?[8] In trying to determine the best, or even a possible, match between community and worship, it will be important to try and avoid thinking in subjective generalizations about what people like or don't like, such as young people don't like pews or old people don't like live bands. Such generalizations are seldom true and actively prevent recognition of what God has already been doing in the Church.

Marcus Ramshaw, the initiator of the Goth Eucharist in Cambridge, states that three-quarters of the people that come to the service are actually confirmed. He sees them as the sheep that got away, not the black sheep of the family.

> As a priest I discovered a lot of my friends were still fascinated by the supernatural and fascinated by the Christian faith. And I actually wanted to find a way of creating a service in which they felt they weren't going to be judged by what they wore or their attitudes and where taboo subjects such as depression or self harming or suicidal thoughts or grief, actually were talked about in an honest way in the same way that say the psalmist does.[9]

Pioneeer ministers are called to work outside of the confines of the Church, to be free to seek the lost who seldom, if ever, enter a church. But once they have found them, often the only place that they can bring them home rejoicing is to buildings that are owned by the Church.[10] In many small towns and villages, or even large city centres, the local church is the only landlord with rooms to let at reasonable rents, with all the facilities and resources needed to host a small experimental gathering. One of the best reasons for hosting a fresh expression of church inside a church is that it is obvious from the start that what is happening is about church – it is about gathering together to explore the

boundary between earth and heaven and the reality of the presence of God here, not just 'up there'.

There are people who have argued against hosting a fresh
expression of church in a church. They do so on the grounds that
the time-honoured symbols of the church, its atmosphere of
prayer and the undisputed presence of God, can 'put people off'
or even intimidate the unchurched. Such arguments have merit
only if it is believed that humans have any control over how God
is known or experienced. God is awesome. Honesty is surely the
best policy? There is no such thing as 'God-lite'. No matter how
competent the pioneer or fresh expression practitioner, God
cannot be dumbed down. God is God. God is holy, and the spaces
where humans encounter God are holy precisely because humans
are called to be holy. There is no way to disguise that and still
hold on to the truth that God is not like us.

It is not the task of a fresh expression of church to persuade
people to believe in a 'tame' God. Church-lite is not to be confused with God-lite. In church-lite, every effort is made to minimize the unnecessary and unfamiliar components of worship. It
is possible, for example, to minimize the liturgy of the Church,
to cut down the length of an act of worship, to not wear clerical
robes, chant psalms or use incense, and yet still invite people to
pray, to encounter God by drawing near and walking on holy
ground. Reducing the structured formality of the worship of the
Church should never be done with the intention of minimizing
the impact of the presence of God.

The counter to the argument that church has little in common
with the poor, or the marginalized, the busy or the retired is that
it was designed to lift people from such states, to give them a glimpse
of something other, something more:

> The tragedy of modern urban life is not only that so many in our
> cities are oppressed and powerless, but also that so many have noth-
> ing surrounding them in which any human being could possibly
> take sensory delight. For this state of affairs we who are Christians
> are as guilty as any.[11]

All church space should clearly communicate a sense of spirituality, of the holiness of God and of the ultimate purpose of the

building. The primary criteria used for discerning which room in a church is best suited for a fresh expression of church should be:

- The attractiveness of the room for the task for which it is intended.
- The way in which the room communicates a sense of the holy.
- The availability of the room.

The following illustrations show how the criteria can be applied:

1 **3 into 1** (a fresh expression which teaches cookery to parents to enable them to prepare three good meals a day for a family on a tight budget).
   Attractiveness: Good-sized kitchen and a comfortable room which can be set up as a crèche. Kitchen – well equipped and meeting statutory regulations concerning food preparation.
   Communication: Unobtrusive Christian art around the walls, classical or contemporary Christian background music. Children's Bible story posters in the crèche area.
   Availability: Any weekday during term-time.
2 **TxT** (a fresh expression which reaches out to unchurched teenagers).
   Attractiveness: Minimum of two rooms, plus sanctuary space. Large brightly lit games room, and smaller comfortable lounge with subdued lighting. Games room/sports hall, well lit, good size, hard floor, suitable for ball games, football, table tennis, etc.; lounge set as youth sanctuary with bean bags, sofas, easy chairs and floor space, etc. Sanctuary space: room for table/altar, floor space or chairs, subdued lighting; ambient digital projection.
   Communication: Christian posters/graffiti on the walls of the games room. Lounge to be lit softly – cross, Bible or simple prayer space set up as a visual in one corner. Sanctuary to be warm, with subdued lighting. Candles preferred.
   Availability: Any weeknight evening.
3 **P T and JC** (a fresh expression parent and toddler club which has progressed to include a ten-minute act of worship at the end of the session).

Attractiveness: One large room, kitchen space, plus sanctuary space. Large brightly lit room, for children's play area. Kitchen space sufficient to prepare tea/coffee and children's drinks. Sanctuary space needs to be well lit, warm, clear floor space.

Communication: Children's Bible story posters/artwork for walls of main meeting room. Simple sanctuary space, table/altar with plain cross and Bible. Piano or keyboard if possible.

Availability: Morning or afternoon any weekday or Saturday.

Knowing that each room, either deliberately or subliminally, is communicating some aspect of the gospel reminds the church to be good stewards of its premises. The state of every one of its rooms is as important as the altar or communion table, for they can all be used by God as a means of grace to communicate the presence of Christ. Sacred time and space are the two fundamental dimensions hidden away as inessential compared to values. Unless time and space are made, there can be no opportunity for the church to become the sacrament of ordinary, public life.[12] Church aesthetics matter. Certain sights, symbols, sounds and even smells are associated with spirituality and holiness in people's minds.

The craze for the modern contemporary clean and bright multi-purpose utilitarian worship space has all but passed. A significant number of young people today will admit, when they are actually asked, that they are more likely to feel close to God in what they consider to be 'authentic' sacred spaces such as cathedrals and even cemeteries. Research has shown that the more time people spend in the 'virtual' worlds of computers, TV, theatre and cinema, the more importance they tend to place on 'actual reality' and on authenticity which they can measure in terms of age, history, permanence, and atmosphere. The multi-sensory impact of a well maintained and much-loved sanctuary space or traditional church can offer this authenticity that is so sought after, in a way that a multi-purpose building, dressed for worship one day a week, simply cannot.

Although fresh expressions of church often engage in alternative forms of worship, they seldom need or want to create alternative sacred spaces. Existing church spaces are frequently lit or used differently, often more creatively, but they are seldom permanently altered. Cathedral crypts, for example, are popular places for reflective 'alternative' worship, as are church naves, bell towers, lady chapels, altar spaces and even galleries. In these fresh expressions of church, designed to cater for what are known as 'seeker' congregations, candles, ambient lighting or projections, music, incense are all frequently used to draw the attention of the worshippers to the signs and symbols of the sanctuary. The purpose of such reflective worship is usually to heighten the awareness of the presence of God by opening the senses to that which is holy.

Consider, for example, the once-a-month service led by the Revd Philip Roderick, called Contemplative Fire. This is an act of worship attended by around 80 people which is held in a twelfth-century monastic chapel in a Buckinghamshire hamlet. Describing them as part of a regular sequence of local gatherings for 'stillness and storytelling, the playful as well as the profound', Philip says that the services are in keeping with an 'open Catholic tradition'. They include procession, the use of incense, movement, body prayer and visual icons. They 'celebrate the sacrament of the present moment in the beauty of nature, liturgy and teaching'. They are an excellent example of how fresh expressions can sit comfortably within existing traditional church buildings that are prepared to play to their strengths and to their history. Contemplative Fire is, according to its leader, a deliberate attempt 'to blend ancient and modern, a deep journey to meet Jesus, the one who transforms our consciousness'. It was deliberately aimed at 'people who can't do traditional God language' and are put off by modern church structures. In spite of its unlikely venue, Contemplative Fire is gaining converts and introducing those who would not normally attend church to the richness of the mystical experience of the Eucharist in such a holy setting. 'It is amazing', says Philip, 'how many people who are not Christians are delighted that the Church of England is hosting traditions which honour the contemplative and mystical.'[13]

Seeker church and Contemplative Fire worship attempts to do much more than simply indulge the senses. By inviting people to a planned and staged exploration of holy signs and places, it encourages people to discover and encounter God in the holy places in their own lives. It reintroduces the concept of timely personal discovery, of God's unfolding love, to a generation more used to having everything pre-packaged and ready to go.

When a fresh expression of church seeks to offer an alternative form of worship which does entail changing the configuration of a worship space to accommodate a worship band, sound system and/or digital projection equipment, every effort must be made to ensure that whatever changes are made to the sanctuary are in keeping with the architecture and the theology of the sacred space. Even churches that were not built in the Middle Ages, and which do not have choir stalls or bell towers, steeples or naves, still have a theology of sacred space. Regardless of the denomination, it is safe to presume that all purpose-built churches were designed with care as a means of communicating the word of God. Every aspect of their shape, the placement of the permanent furniture, the size of the entrance hall, the placement of the congregation relative to the communion area or worship dais, even, in some instances, the direction in which the church will face, were all originally designed by an architect on behalf of a community of faith to communicate in three dimensions the good news of God with us.

One consequence of the care with which they were designed is that it is possible for the smallest unwitting change to sacred space to alter profoundly the impact of the original message. In one church, for example, the worship platform was quite small. So, on most Sundays, the communion table was pushed behind the organ bench. What seemed quite natural and practical at the time, however, was quite disturbing to others.

> hiding our communion table non-verbally communicated (though maybe only subconsciously for many) that we did not value the Lord's Supper. It looked like Jesus' institution of the sacrament had no place in our worship, except on the Sundays we actually took communion.[14]

As fresh expressions of church are concerned with providing worship for those who are predominantly unchurched and unfamiliar with Christian customs and theology, it becomes even more important to rethink worship and how exclusive it can be.

One particular mixed-economy church was keen to meet the members of a fresh expression that they were supporting and so invited them to a church carol service. It soon became all too apparent how exclusive church can be for the unchurched. Charity Hamilton explains:

> They all arrived bang on the start time, instead of the unwritten rule about arriving 15 minutes before, they sat at the front as one would do at a gig. The seventeen-year-old next to me turned to me and said, 'Charity, what's this?' I looked down and realized she was talking about the big blue hymn book she'd been handed on the way in. I turned round to them all, held up the book, and said, 'Listen, it's a bit like karaoke, OK? The bloke at the front with the outfit on will shout out a number, we look it up then sing it'![15]

The theology of the visual impact of worship also needs to be considered. Does what is happening make it appear as though Jesus is not as important as something else? For example, while it may be perfectly correct for a rock band to play on a raised platform with the adoring fans standing singing along below, it sends completely the wrong message for a worship band to do the same thing in a church. The congregation have not gathered as fans of the band and worship is not a staged performance. The theology of the Church should never be allowed to be compromised by the ill-thought-out positioning of worship leaders, whether they are musicians, preachers or healers. Most churches were designed to place Christ centre-stage and to facilitate the liturgy of the Church. Christ is present in the gathered people and in the symbols of the cross, or the communion table/altar or the open Word. Those who are seeking to bring people to Christ should think hard before wanting to replace or 'upstage' any or all of these symbols with something else, particularly something as transient as a music group or a guest preacher, or a projector screen.

It is possible, although obviously more expensive, to fit modern communications equipment into a church so that it is all but invisible when not in use, and does not intrude into the sanctity of the worship when it is. Projectors can be housed considerately, either high up out of normal view or in custom-made cabinets designed to blend in with the rest of the church furniture. Projector screens can be back-lit, for example, and set deliberately to one side. If it has been perfectly acceptable for centuries for a pulpit to be set to one side in the church in order not to obscure the centrality of Christ, then surely the same must be true of the preacher's digital replacement! It is surprising how, all too often, those who set up the audio-visual equipment in their churches fail to notice how intrusive the loops of cables, black speakers and metal stands can be in a room full of white worn stone and polished oak, designed to be lit by sunlight pouring through stained glass. Even in modern churches with soft furnishings and bright open spaces, such equipment usually looks glaringly out of place unless it has been deliberately designed to blend in. It is always worth the extra time and cost that it takes to make the technology as unobtrusive as possible.

Care with aesthetics can make all the difference to enabling people to worship, especially if worship is something new to them.

The only way of ensuring that any worship will achieve its desired outcome is by prioritizing God. When setting the space for worship, the questions are not 'Can the screen be seen?' but 'Can God be seen?' – 'Will the preacher be heard?' but 'Will God be heard?'

People are often far more forgiving than worship leaders and pioneers are inclined to believe, when it comes to participating in an act of worship. More importantly, those who are being introduced to the faith through a fresh expression in a church are more likely to respond positively to Christ when they are able to see others treat the symbols of his living presence and his house with deliberate courtesy and respect.

7

Common boundaries

So let us not grow weary in doing what is right, for we will reap at harvest time, if we do not give up. So then, whenever we have an opportunity, let us work for the good of all, and especially for those of the family of faith.   (Gal. 6.9–10)

Holding on to existing congregations while pioneering new expressions of church takes tact and diplomacy. It also needs clear boundaries to be set for good theological and spiritual reasons. This chapter focuses on helping existing congregations identify what is sacred and special to them for their own sake so that they can learn to coexist with alternative forms of church without fear.

Pioneer ministers are unlikely to increase the size of an existing congregation. Fresh expressions of church will not lead to a growth in the regular Sunday service. On the other hand, a fresh expression of church may eventually replace the existing congregation, and a pioneer minister may leave a church once the new initiative has become fully self-funding. If church members consider this to be unfair or unjust then they should urgently ask the church to reconsider why it is interested in becoming a mixed-economy church. The answer will hopefully be, for Christ's sake.

Participating in the ongoing mission of the Church was easier when the mission was conducted in another country and to another people. This was a form of mission that people felt they understood and could relate to. When the mission is on the doorstep, however, it can be confusing, especially when the minister announces that the grand purpose of undertaking the mission is not necessarily to encourage more people to come to the church that they currently minister to. Existing congregations can quickly feel neglected and used rather than co-workers in the vineyard or participants in the kingdom. What is helpful, especially in the early stages of becoming a mixed-economy church, are clear, well defined boundaries. These are not lines that must never be crossed, God forbid! Rather they are lines of intent, which mark out the scope of the hopes and aspirations of the mission and which afford some definition and framework for what is understandably a somewhat risky venture. They are not created to delineate between the fresh expression and the existing congregation. They help to identify the common ground, the places of the mutual accountability before God which is at the heart of all church unity. To that extent, they are common boundaries, established for the sake of mission and ministry. Negotiating and agreeing these boundaries together should form the basis for a renewable covenant relationship between the church and the fresh expression, or work of the pioneer minister. This covenant should, where possible, be written down, not in legal jargon, but in terms of the values and principles used to determine where the boundaries should be set.

In most places, a mixed-economy church seldom simply shares its premises with a fresh expression of church or hosts a pioneer ministry. In practice, the same church leaders, lay and ordained, are involved with both the inherited and the exploratory forms of ministry. The PCC, or church council, usually have oversight of the projects as an item on their agenda, and there is generally some form of financial understanding about the new arrangements. The shared or common boundaries are therefore:

- spatial – the use of the building
- financial – the use of church funds
- chronological – the use of church time
- spiritual – the use of the church theology
- ministerial – the use of the priest's or minister's time.

Spatial boundaries

The previous chapter provided some guidelines about how a church could examine the existing use of its space and discern its suitability for mixed-economy ministry. Once one or two forms of fresh expression of church are happening on a regular basis within the church, however, other issues quickly come to the fore and can be a real source of contention if the spatial boundaries are not established in advance. The determinative boundary question here is, 'What space will we invest in mixed-economy mission?'

The question can of course be answered on many levels, as space can mean location as well as rooms within a building, but to deal with the more likely scenario first, the question could be answered by a formal licence-to-let arrangement between the church and the fresh expression or pioneer minister.

A licence to let is a fully documented letting arrangement which sets out unambiguously which rooms and spaces the church will make available at what time and under what conditions. It defines who is responsible for the upkeep and state of repair of the rooms, the storage space and any associated parking spaces. It also stipulates who is legally responsible for the provision of such things as liability insurance as well as defining the minimum child safety precautions, for example, which have to be adhered to. Above all this it also stipulates what the use of the rooms will cost, when the invoices must be paid, and how much notice is required to terminate the agreement.

However, while a formal licence to let might seem like a good, clean way of defining spatial boundaries, it should be avoided unless it is absolutely necessary. A licence to let allows the church to treat a fresh expression of church or pioneer ministry in the same way that it would a secular pre-school or photography club. This can lead to an independence which pushes at the boundaries of what is meant by church unity.

A more helpful way of defining spatial boundaries would be to agree on the nature and extent of the sacred space and on how it should be respected by everyone in order to enable the worship of God and the nurture and care of God's people to happen. It is more helpful for example for a fresh expression which includes a shared meal prepared on the premises to know in advance that lingering cooking smells permeating the sanctuary might be deemed disrespectful than to simply be told that they can't eat in the church. Knowing why space is being protected or reserved allows it to be willingly respected.

Even if it is not possible or desirable to share building space there may still be spatial boundaries to be negotiated and agreed. There has been a tendency in the past for churches to jealously guard their locality and to assume that they have the exclusive or natural right to the care of souls within a particular parish or area. Ecumenical progress has, to a large extent, ended the illusion of the one church per parish, but the mentality sometimes persists, preventing the church from working in partnership with other churches or even ministers in mission. The new Bishops' Mission Orders now make it possible for Church of England priests and pioneer ministers to initiate new ministries and plant churches across parish boundaries as well as work ecumenically on such ventures. British Methodist ministers have no spatial boundaries that need to be circumvented or legislated for, although the circuit is recognized as the primary focus for mission.

The difficulty does not arise from the legislation, but in the heart of the existing membership. Research has demonstrated how, in most instances over the last ten years, new church plants have grown more by transfer than by conversion. They have drawn members from existing Christian congregations rather than by evangelism. Pioneer ministry is intended to be different. It is intended as mission primarily to the unchurched rather than the churched or dechurched (by which is meant those who once had a church affiliation but who for some reason or another have ceased to attend). The intent is clear, but the outcome is not: is the church willing to take the risk? Is the church willing to provide support for an alternative ministry to be established in the community in which it finds itself, even knowing that those who respond will be unlikely to see themselves as connected with the sponsoring church in any way? Defining the boundary of where a pioneer might work and entering into a covenant relationship is a good way of helping the membership to own up to their fears as well as to identify their hopes for the intended ministry.

Financial boundaries

As congregations in defined churches have dwindled, so has their income. In many parts of the country, the weekly offering is drawn almost entirely from the generosity of pensioners. It can be hard enough to maintain the church building as it is, without having to make changes or update it to suit an experimental form of church which offers no guarantee of any financial return. It is not difficult to see why finance can be a real source of friction. The defining question for establishing this boundary is, 'How much money is this church prepared to invest in mixed-economy mission?' Again, the question can be answered in various ways. Financially speaking, the most helpful answer is to agree a percentage formula rather than a fixed amount of the church's annual budget. This enables most people in the church to appreciate the extent of the commitment being made to mixed economy without necessarily being able to read a financial statement. It also allows fluctuations in the church's finances to be automatically shared with the exploratory mission of the church. Whatever figure or percentage is agreed upon, it should be based on a proper assessment of the costs.

This should include:

- the cost of any new or specialized equipment required
- the cost of any refurbishments or modifications required
- the cost of the room hire (based on lost rental charges if the room had been available to any other organization – this then incorporates heating and lighting costs)
- the cost of any staff time on a pro-rata basis (include the clergy as well as admin. staff)
- the cost of any consumables on a weekly or monthly basis
- communications costs.

Once the costs are known, the church can enter into realistic dialogue with the pioneer concerning the planned ministry, *but it should be the theology of the ministry, not the cost, which should be allowed to provide the answer to this boundary question.*

The theological answer to the boundary question will have to wrestle hard with the Scriptures, which make it perfectly clear that it is not possible to serve God and money. Finances are important for ministry, but they do not dictate its success. God does. The Church began with no money and no buildings; it replicates itself repeatedly through the efforts of those called by God to pioneer new ways of being church that are similarly begun without funds and without buildings. The disciples were sent out with explicit instructions to take nothing for the journey – no staff, no bag, no bread, no money, no extra tunic (Luke 9.3). This injunction forced them to be dependent on God's provision for the future of the ministry, and to enter into those sorts of relationships that would enable them to ask for and receive help in sustaining the ministry. One of the problems with mixed-economy ministry is that it is harder to realize how much can be done with how little. Church members have become accustomed to thinking in terms of clergy stipends and expenses, heating and lighting bills, building maintenance, administration costs, denominational levies, and so on – all the bills that arise as a direct consequence of owning buildings and being church in the usual manner.

Pioneer ministry, however, may never coalesce into a regular physical, visible ministry. It may never need to own its own premises, or pay the stipend of a regular minister. It may be content to be part of the mixed economy which allows it to share in the generosity of other churches for its sacramental worship, but otherwise meet in homes, or cafés, or shops or libraries, or skating rinks or in cyberspace. This means that it will never know the burden of such bills, but it also means that it seldom has a regular collection either, or any other means of generating a regular income. Pioneering ministry cannot be guaranteed to ever provide the hosting church with a financial return on its investment, not even in terms of an increase in the size of the church's congregation. The success of pioneering ministry tends to be measured more by the impact that is made on the community than on the number of people who attend worship or put money in a hat. It is measured in friends won for Jesus, not in bums on pews or communicants at the table.

So what financial boundaries are common to both the pioneer and the church? The church and the pioneer are linked by a relationship that has been forged by God's generous grace. It is worth remembering that the early Christians needed help from the established church of their time in order to reach the world. A careful reading of the Acts of the Apostles shows that they attended the synagogue wherever they were and went to the temple at festival times. They used the resources that God had put at their disposal, in the same way that pioneer ministers today want to. The church may be able to provide the shelter that the pioneer asks for, or simply the ecclesial hospitality that the new community may need. If the pioneer is the one who is called to 'go sell all you have and come and follow me', then perhaps the church is the body called to provide the gracious hospitality and provision that God has promised will be provided.

Chronological boundaries

Time is money, according to the best marketing strategists; in church life, however, it can often seem to be far more limited and expensive! A frighteningly large number of congregations describe themselves as elderly, as though that says something important about the state of their souls before God or their commitment to mission. The only thing that seems to have direct bearing on the age of the congregation is the time that they feel they have to give to something new; they would like to see a project bear fruit in their lifetime. The defining question for this boundary is therefore: 'How much time will the church invest in mixed-economy mission?'

Mark's Gospel has an amazing sense of urgency running through it. The word 'immediately' occurs so many times that it can seem as though Jesus was on a race to get to the cross. Christian mission often has that same sense of urgency, but it needs to be held in balance with a deep awareness of God's time. Jesus might have been in a race for the short three years of his earthly ministry, but that ministry only began when God was ready – 'in the fullness of time'. In the same way, the church needs to be prepared to invest whatever time it takes to prepare for mission, rather than rushing into things and trying out the first pioneering project it encounters that seems to have worked elsewhere. Mission and ministry are about the creation, development and enjoyment of three-way relationships between God, the community and the church. Relationships take time to form, more time to develop and as much time as possible to be enjoyed. The

Church often tries to move through this natural process far too quickly, and then wonders why the relationships that it forms don't last.

Christ's incarnational ministry teaches the Church that the time spent before and after mission is often significantly longer than that spent in mission. The time before mission is the time of discernment, of simply loving God's people, of getting to know them and value them for who they are. It is the time of listening to the cry of God's people, and seeing the injustice and apathy that distorts the kingdom and prevents God's offer of salvation, of an alternative community from being heard. This is the time when ministers are prepared. Only when they have truly seen, only when they are really aware of the need and the potential, only when they are so convinced that they are called by God to address the needs they have been shown does the 'before time' end and the time of ministry begin. By which time, they will generally know what God wants them to do. The time of prayerful preparation enables the church to discern whether they are called to start a new ministry themselves, or support someone else that God has sent to them in answer to their prayers, or both.

The second question of time then becomes more urgent – how long should the time of ministry be? There is little consensus in the Church as to how long a pioneer ministry needs to be nurtured before it can and should be sustained by others. The average time seems to be around three to five years. The Methodist connexional pioneering minister's scheme, for example, expects the connexion to 'Support the projects for an extended period (full support for 5 years, partial support for a further five years).'[1] In the opinion of the project coordinators, 'The less a project has in common with our "normal" church experience, the longer it will take to grow to self-sufficiency.' Independent research from the USA, where pioneering ministry has been happening a little longer under the guise of church plants and emerging church, suggests that the shorter the time the better. Whatever time is agreed upon, it needs to then be added to the preparation time.

Before the final answer to the time-boundary question can be determined, however, the amount of 'ascension time' needs to be discerned. What is the role of the pioneer and the mixed-economy church when the time of active ministry is at an end, and the mission moves on to the third decisive time of entrusting and releasing? The pioneer role is to progressively but deliberately leave within an agreed time-scale so that the work of God can continue past the point where it is focused in the work of one individual or team. The church's role, however, is less time-constrained. The church's task is to assist in this process by enabling the fresh expression of church that it has nurtured to discover and own what is distinctive and Spirit-filled about its work and to grow in confidence to the extent that it can be self-replicating. This is the time when the relationship can be enjoyed, and hence there is no real need to end it. The church should simply be encouraged to begin the threefold cycle of preparation, ministry and releasing again, knowing that it has helped to answer one of the community's needs for God.

Spiritual boundaries

The gospel that we have to proclaim is the product of fresh expressions of church: just as Christianity can be thought of as a fresh expression of Judaism, so the Gentile church pioneered by Paul and Silas and others was a fresh expression of the apostolic church in Jerusalem. As the council at Jerusalem makes clear, the process of contextualization and inculturation does not always happen smoothly. Disputes about doctrine and practice inevitably surface. What is right before God for one community may not be right for another, but who should decide – and how? Most churches have a mission statement that they review on a periodic basis. The defining question for this boundary is, 'How will this church set the limits of inculturation?'

In the words of Bishop Dr Michael Nazir-Ali, 'This process of inculturation must go on.' But, he said, there are limits to this process: whatever the process of inculturation does or does not do, it cannot compromise. It cannot compromise how God has revealed himself to the world, how Jesus Christ has come in the flesh, what he has done, who he is.

We are faced, in a changing situation, where people want to be Church with those who are like them. We find it in Africa, where people want to be Church in the context of their own tribe; we find it in Asia, and now we find it with the affinity Churches, the network Churches, and the virtual Churches in the North.

He had once been hostile to this tendency, but his study of the household churches, he said, had led him to modify his views a little, and he now thought it permissible.

But there is one condition, and that is that this is not the only way to be Church. If you want to be Church with those who are like you, you also have to be Church with those who are unlike you.[2]

Being a mixed-economy church means finding a way of living out the unity that the Church aspires to every day. It means learning to live with the difference in practice and even perhaps in theology in such a way that the gospel of Christ is able to be heard loud and clear above and within the sounds of healthy discussion and debate. But there should be limits, and the church will need to decide in advance what those are. Most churches will be content with their denominational safeguards on such matters, recognizing that the Church is a broad church, which allows for and actively encourages theological diversity as a healthy sign of Christian discourse. If the fresh expression is being led by someone who has been ordained, then they will be under the discipline of the Church for the conduct of the worship and the gospel that they proclaim. If the pioneering ministry is lay led, then the church can invite the pioneers to submit to either clerical oversight or oversight by the church council. The oversight should be offered as a gift, not a requirement. It was Paul's choice to submit to the will of the council, for the sake of the unity of the Church. If the council had repeatedly asked Paul to attend and account for his teachings and practices, the Bible would undoubtedly look very different today.

Some churches will not be comfortable housing experimental expressions of church that sit lightly to, or perhaps even contravene, the theological or ecclesiological core values which they believe help to define them. If this is the case then it is almost certain that those core values will already exist in the form of a mission statement which could be offered as the church's answer to this particular boundary question. While this would be an understandable and perfectly acceptable choice to make, it is somewhat contradictory to the spirit of a mixed-economy approach to church. Pioneer ministry is risky, it will result in changes to the church and perhaps even to the church's theology, but this has always been the case – thank God. Without pioneers like Paul, all men would still be being circumcised. Without pioneering ministry, the Church would still be meeting on the Sabbath and not on Sunday; without pioneers like Cranmer, Wesley, Newman, Booth, and their like, the Church would not be what it is today. Without pioneers like those needing space in the Church, the Church of tomorrow might not be like anything at all.

The Council of Jerusalem provides a good model for churches uncertain about the limits of inculturation. If and when it is felt that there is a serious significant difference that could lead to a division in the unity of the church, then invite discussion and prayer on the matter. Lay out the dispute clearly: what is it about really? Be prepared to ask:

- How does this difference enable those who experience it to draw near to Christ?
- Is it a genuine adaptation, inspired by the Spirit so that people are able to worship God?
- What evidence is there of this?

The questions should always be directed towards identifying the benefits of the difference to the people it directly affects, rather than finding ways of settling the unease of the people that it is not addressed to.

Had the council at Jerusalem listened only to the Pharisees who were unsettled by the fact that Gentile Christians were not behaving according to the Mosaic law, the Church would be very different today. The bold honesty of Peter concerning the difficulty of trying to keep the law that they as Jews were called to keep is worth hearing afresh. Has our ecclesiology made it too difficult for people to come to faith? Have the rules and regulations governing our conduct of worship, our access to the sacraments, our sharing in fellowship, actively prohibited people from meeting with the God we adore? The key test in discerning the validity of a spiritual difference of a pioneering ministry should never be, 'Would we do, or agree with, what is happening here?' but 'Is there evidence of the Holy Spirit at work here?'

Ministerial boundaries

Often when churches begin to explore mission they do so with the expectation that mission is the minister's task. It is certainly true that most ministers who are 'highly motivated, sensitive, passionate, caring, longing to be used effectively in the service of the gospel of God – signed up so that they could make a difference'.[3] Very few of those who entered the priesthood did so in order to spend their time as pastoral or social workers, building maintenance engineers, untrained child minders and teachers and committee chairs. Yet a significantly large number of clergy and professional lay people now believe that they are not expected or able to engage in mission. When pushed to explain, most point to the constraints on their time caused by the existing demands of their congregations. The defining question for this boundary is therefore 'What ministerial resources will this church commit to a mixed-economy mission?'

Not all ministerial resources are ordained – ministry is the work of the whole people of God, but all ministry done in the name of the Church needs to be recognized and owned as such. The ministry of the local preacher or reader, churchwarden or steward, treasurer and pastoral secretary is as vital to the pioneer ministry of a mixed-economy church as that of the deacon or priest, curate or minister. It is also worth noting that not all ministers are called to participate in mission, or able to. If every ordained minister were, as is often suggested, a pioneer minister, then the Church would be in a very different place today. It may be that the majority of those who are ordained also feel called to pioneer ministry, but the demands on their time to maintain what has become an almost universally expected parish-style pastoral ministry prevents all but the most workaholic from succeeding. One solution suggested by a younger minister hints at the root of the problem: he discovered that it was much easier to ask for forgiveness than it was to seek permission. It is not that ministers lack either passion or ability or even entrepreneurial or leadership skills, what they seem to lack most is the permission they believe they need from their congregations and denominations to minister other than as their predecessors did before them, that is, as expected.

The issue of ministerial time has become ever more pressing as the number of those willing to serve in the Church has declined along with the rest of the church membership. The increase in the number of paid lay employees in the churches is indicative of an underlying disassociation of discipleship and service. This has largely been caused by the frenzied pace of modern living. When both parents work all week and try to raise a family, it seems harsh to expect them to also serve as a pastoral carer or assist on a soup run. Everyone is busy, too busy to pioneer a fresh expression of church. The direct consequence of this is that before any form of ministry can be committed to mission it needs first to be released from what else it is already actively engaged in. This, of course, is the real dilemma because this demands nothing less than that the church and the ministers rethink their use of time and energy in the light of their answer to the fundamental question driving the entire mission agenda – what is church for?

If church exists primarily so that Christians can worship God, then it makes perfect sense for the ministerial time of the church to be focused on the preparation and celebration of the liturgy. This would mean that the church expects others to engage with the task of mission – of making new Christians. This is based on a 'come to us' understanding of church. If however, church exists as the body of Christ to continue Christ's ministry of reconciliation, then the ministerial time of the church should be focused on those who are not yet reconciled rather than on those who are. Those who have, as a result of the church's ministry, found faith by grace should be encouraged to grow in that grace. This would mean not just attending worship but taking up their role within the ministry of the body of Christ. A church of predominantly passive worshippers is not a church at all. Stuart Murray Williams writes:

Excessive time spent by staff and volunteers running their church rather than engaging in mission beyond their church is rightly regarded as selfish (as well as being institutional suicidal in a post-Christendom context). We should stop complaining that 80% of the work needed to run a church is done by 20% of the people: 20% of the people should be ample, releasing the rest to get on with mission.[4]

One of the most difficult questions for a congregation to wrestle with concerning ministerial boundaries is how the sacraments should be celebrated. There is something timeless and essential about the celebration of the Eucharist which demands a respect throughout Christendom. Although there is no universal agreement concerning who may and who may not lead a congregation in the celebration of the Lord's Supper, the importance of this sacrament to the mission and the life of the Church is seldom disputed. Holy Communion is not simply an act of worship, and a fresh expression of the sacraments needs to take into consideration the fact that the structure, form and many of the words of the liturgy are considered by many to be the gift of God to the whole of the Church and one of its most important visible expressions of unity.

It is not enough therefore to talk about the Church having missional values of Trinity, incarnation, hospitality and so on if in the next breath eucharistic community is seen reductively as a worship style, or restrictively as a blueprint to be avoided for the sake of mission. In so doing the whole incarnational grammar of the Church is debased.[5]

One form of ministerial resource that a mixed-economy church may need to invest in therefore is the sacramental. While it might be difficult for a lay pioneer or a deacon to accept the necessity of the 'priestly' ministry for sacramental worship, it is one of the ways by which a new community can be opened up to the mystery of God and encouraged to focus less on the person leading and more on the gift of God being given. The ritual practices of the church community, far from being extrinsic to the Church's being, are actually the way in which individuals and society at large gain access to the mystery of faith.[6] Leadership of a fresh expression of church does not grant the right to preside at the Lord's table, or to baptize in the name of the Father, Son and Holy Spirit. This 'authority' or privilege can only be granted by the whole of the Church in whose name it is undertaken. Pioneers unwilling to draw on the sacramental resources of the ministry of the mixed-economy church need seriously to consider whether they are themselves called to ordained or authorized ministry or whether they are simply being unnecessarily over-protective of God's people. The sacraments make God present to the community, not the priest or the presiding minister.

8

Harvest

According to Dr John Sentamu, if a fresh expression was genuinely established for and largely attracted the unchurched then the church and its leaders will face two key issues in the coming years:

First, how can they make the transition from community-based initiatives to fully responsible sacramental congregations in their own right, nurturing life-long disciples of Christ?

Secondly, as they grow and become settled into a style and way of being and working that is effective for them, how can they maintain their mission imperative?[1]

As he rightly points out, the second question is one that should be addressed by all churches, whether experimental or existent; the challenge of maintaining the necessary energy and commitment levels for mission should not be underestimated.

His first question is the one that is the most challenging for a mixed-economy church. While he and others are working to find the answers to these questions, mixed-economy churches must be more proactive in their planning and preparation for the day when the pioneering ministry that they have nurtured and supported has begun to form its own unique identity and make its own positive contribution to the broader identity of the Christian Church. The problem with Dr Sentamu's question is that it demonstrates a failure to recognize the extent to which fresh expressions of church are different. Thinking outside the box with regard to mission and ministry means that not only are the normal visible parameters for 'church' changed, so too are the parameters for measuring 'success' or 'failure'. For a church plant, success would usually mean that the church did become a fully sacramental congregation its own right, that it was able to sustain itself financially. A successful church is one that is well on the way to becoming a self-ish church, self-governing, self-financing and self-reproducing (although in practice few go on to achieve the third!). But are those appropriate parameters for measuring 'success' in a pioneer ministry or a fresh expression of church?

Perhaps one of the most significant differences between church in the twenty-first century and that of the last will be the way in which it is governed or financed. Working with a theology of interdependence rather than independence, a fresh expression of church might choose to remain as a child of the Church, always dependent on the host church for some aspects of its life, such as the sacraments. Will this make it less 'success-ful'? Pioneers repeatedly point out that the members of network churches are usually part of several different networks. They do not necessarily hold to the same idea of sacramental community. Receiving the sacraments together in one place is not deemed to be essential, as they recognize that they are bound to each other through the sacrament, the body of Christ, not their locality or physicality. Similarly, many network-based fresh expressions of church, particularly those that are internet- or cell-church-based, manage to exist, grow and replicate without any recognizable 'government' or independent finances. Members pay their own way, there are no overheads as the church meets online, or in people's homes, there are no clergy stipends to pay as this is a church of the laity for the laity, there are no building costs, yet the cells continue to multiply. How will the success or failure of such churches or ministries be measured?

The definition of a fresh expression used at the start of this book says that every fresh expression will have the potential to become a mature expression of church. This does not mean that it must end up looking like a typical circuit or parish church. It does mean that it will be a recognizable and self-confessed part of the one holy catholic and apostolic Church of Christ.

Provided that a fresh expression of church was founded with that ultimate objective in mind, to be able to take its place in the mixed economy of church that is the body of Christ in the twenty-first century, then regardless of how 'alternative' it may look, or be, it will still be possible to measure whether or not it is growing and developing as it should.

A ministry will be growing and developing as it should if:

- It is continuing to form community and make disciples of Jesus Christ of those who are unchurched, assisting them to grow in grace and holiness.
- It is raising up new leadership from within its number to share in the goals of the fledgling church.
- It is continuing to adapt and work through the consequences of inculturation for the specific context that it has been called to serve in such a way that the gospel is able to be heard and responded to.
- It is finding ways to express the gifts of the Holy Spirit as they are shared among the new community and the fruits of those gifts are recognizable to others as the outworking of the grace of God in the lives of those concerned.
- It is continuing to serve the community to which it is called to be the presence of Christ, such that the community is being transformed by kingdom values.

Accordingly, a ministry will be clearly failing if:

- It is becoming a holy huddle or a churchy clique rather than a gospel community.
- It is becoming increasingly dependent on the efforts and energies of the pioneer rather than on Christ.
- It is revising the gospel to suit its own ends.
- It is no longer proclaiming Christ as central to all its endeavours.
- It is becoming more concerned with the style of worship or 'getting it right' than it is about enabling people to know God and be transformed by that knowledge.
- It is no longer looking to find new ways to serve the community as Christ would.

There are of course other tests that could be used, but the criteria given above were chosen because they avoid the usual stereotypes while remaining true to the vision of pioneering ministry as ministry that forms and nurtures Christ-centred communities that are relevant to the cultures and contexts in which they are set.

The failure of a pioneer ministry or fresh expression of church

So what would cause a pioneering ministry or a fresh expression of church to fail? Although the definitions earlier provide some indication, they are only the visible symptoms of the failure rather than the root causes. Drawing on almost 2000 years of church and congregational development, it is possible to identify at least nine key factors that would cause a pioneering ministry to fail.

1 wrong pioneer
2 wrong culture or context
3 lack of training
4 lack of vision
5 lack of focus
6 trying to look 'mature'
7 too much interference from others
8 being unwilling to let go
9 being too heavenly minded to be of any earthly use.

Wrong pioneer

One of the disadvantages of ordained pioneer ministers of the Church of England and Methodist circuit ministers who are engaged in pioneering ministry is that they can be deployed or stationed by someone who the pioneers feel does not fully understand, or is unable to visualize, the ministry that they have been called to. This situation is particularly acute in the Methodist Church at the moment although, as with the Church of England, it is now recognized as an area of serious concern, which the recent Stationing review group has attempted to find ways to address. The situation is further exacerbated by the limited number of paid pioneering posts within the Church. Initial deployment to pioneering posts is, peculiarly, often treated in much the same way as to traditional posts. Every attempt is made to obtain the best possible match between those in the limited pool of pioneer ministers available and the even more limited number of funded posts. What is often forgotten is the strength of the link for some pioneers between context and calling. The constraints that the Church is operating under can often lead to the wrong pioneer being appointed. The question that pioneers have to wrestle with is whether any pioneering appointment will do, or whether they should wait for the right appointment for them.

There is a corresponding problem in the mixed-economy church looking to appoint a pioneer. Churches are often dependent on highly unskilled people to assess the quality and abilities of those who will undertake ministry on their behalf. They are not generally paid professionals, trained in recruitment or psychometric testing. Church interviews are usually conducted by circuit stewards or churchwardens who may have had little or no training in how to determine a candidate's suitability for the post. Traditional ministerial selection is often based on highly subjective factors, such as 'Do we like this person?', 'Do we think she is friendly, agreeable, easy to get along with?', 'Is he known to any of us?', 'Is she warm and outgoing?', 'Could I see myself going to this person with a problem?', 'Does his theology fit with ours?', 'Will she get on with the rest of the congregation?' Most pioneer ministers, however, will have a very different skill set from those best suited to traditional pastoral ministry. They may well present as aggressive, pushy, intense, charismatic and bold rather than accessible, pastoral, supportive and 'nice'. A significant number of pioneers appear to sit lightly to hierarchy and traditional power and control structures. Many could be described as religious introverts, ideally suited to communicate with their sub-culture, but completely ill at ease with the full membership of the Church. It is important to remember that although they are able, few pioneers would be comfortable serving as traditional church ministers, and it is therefore inappropriate to use traditional ministerial criteria to appoint them. This will almost always end up with the wrong pioneer being appointed.

The solution is for both the pioneer and the church to be very clear about the appointment before it begins. A church should never advertise for a pioneer minister or allocate resources for fresh expressions until it knows what it wants (preferably as a result of having undertaken an appraisal of the mission opportunities identified by a recent contextual and cultural survey). The church needs to have identified what skills it needs or expects a pioneer to have, based on the ministry that it expects the pioneer to be able to offer. Pioneers, likewise, need to be able to articulate their calling to pioneer ministry and the skills that they believe that they have developed to enable them to fulfil that calling.

Wrong culture or context

This problem is often created by the same situation stated above with regard to appointment and selection. There is, however, an added dimension that is often overlooked. Pioneering ministry cannot be ministry from outside; it must be ministry from within. The traditional model of church expects the minister to be 'different' from others. Expectations range from 'more religious' and 'better educated' through to 'white male and celibate'! Pioneer ministers, however, are able to minister precisely because they are not 'other' than the community that they are called to minister to. They belong naturally to that community. Pioneering ministry cannot be done to a community by someone who knows what they need; it can only be done with a community by someone who shares in their need. Having a highly educated, middle-aged, middle-class man conduct a pioneering ministry among West End prostitutes is not impossible, but such a ministry conducted by a young woman who has lived most of her life in the shadow of the streets and is aware of what real 'salvation' could mean in that context might have more success at forming community and being seen as a genuinely incarnational presence.

Lack of training

Training for ordained ministry is mandatory in all the main denominations, but not all those who complete ministerial training are appropriately trained for pioneer ministry. It is often the case that lay pioneers who have attended courses in pioneer ministry are better equipped than ordained ministers. What is important is that a church recognizes that pioneer ministry will often take the church into cultures and contexts that are initially unfamiliar. In order to prevent mistakes and to be able to offer full support and encouragement therefore, both the minister and the church should be trained and educated. How, for example, can a church know how to deal with a pioneer ministry to the new asylum seeker community that surrounds it, without receiving appropriate training in how to identify racial prejudice and how to work to lessen or resolve racial tension in the community? Similarly, how can a church genuinely welcome a fresh expression of church for the local HIV and gay community without receiving appropriate training in avoiding sexual discrimination and learning about the ravages of AIDS and the lives of those who suffer from it? A lack of training can all too often lead both the church and the pioneer to make the sort of mistakes that are extremely harmful to ministry, but which are avoidable.

Lack of vision

Pioneer ministry often begins when one trial event has had such success that it is thought worthwhile trying to replicate it. To try and build a pioneer ministry on the success of one afternoon's worship or one meaningful conversation is a really bad idea. Fresh expressions come into being because every context is different. What worked in one place with one group of people of a particular age and gender, race and background may not work the next week or month in a slightly different place with even a slightly different group of people. The vision behind a fresh expression of church is too limited to be sustained if it is not rooted in the continuous call of the gospel to the people of God. Billy Graham's great campaigns, for example, were not successful because they attracted thousands of people to hear him preach, they were successful because of the army of volunteers in the small churches in the countries that he visited following up on the names they were given. The same is true of every great revival. The vision was never to have a rally or preach out in the open; the vision was to make Christians. Pioneering ministry fails when all it can see is the big event, the seeker fair, the creative workshop or the multi-media worship. Ministry is about people, not ideas, spectacles or events.

Lack of focus

In the same way that a lack of vision can effectively kill a fresh expression of church, so too can a lack of focus. In every pioneering situation, the team needs to ask:

- Who is this ministry for?
- How are we trying to conduct this ministry?
- Where is God in what we are doing?
- What are the signs that we will recognize that might indicate to us that the ministry is of God and is effective?

Pioneering is hard work, and in the early days there is often little response. Sometimes this is due to too much hard work being spent on non-essential tasks and not enough being spent actually in the community. Worrying about visible results often leads pioneers to lose focus and try and service the need of the sponsoring church to 'see' something rather than concentrating on the work itself. This is why it is so important for the pioneer to be supported by a team who, by reflecting on the above questions with the pioneer, can help address the needs of the sponsoring bodies for information. The pioneer needs to stay focused on the goal of the ministry and on the call of God to the work as the only sure means of silencing the internal and external pressures for quick and visible returns on the Church's investment.

Trying to look 'mature'

The pressure to 'mature' a fresh expression is considerable, especially if funds for the post are linked to results. One of the consequences is that all too often, pioneers mistakenly think that they need to demonstrate that they have all of the trappings traditionally associated with a successful ministry: a brand name, a web page, even a registered charity number. The cost in terms of time, and money, to say nothing of spiritual integrity, can be disastrous. Neil Cole narrates how one pioneer minister had previously been a successful worship leader. When he started his first 'fresh expression' of church, which met in his living room, he set up a keyboard and sound system, complete with microphone and speakers. 'All ten people heard the songs really well, but it was a little too loud to sing along.'[2] Very few pioneer ministries or fresh expressions of church need the same equipment or resources as a regular church, especially in the early stages. Trying to acquire them, master them, and find a way of using them in a misplaced context, causes loss of focus, and puts an unnecessary strain on what is usually a very limited budget.

Too much interference from others

It is very easy to apportion blame when things go wrong, but sadly many a failure of a pioneer ministry or fresh expression of church can be traced back to too much interference from well-meaning but ill-informed church people. Few of us are aware of how deep-rooted our preconceptions of church actually are, and how they shape and colour our understanding of how ministry should, or should not, be conducted. Sentences that begin 'in my day' may well end in words of wisdom, but are seldom offered as genuine constructive criticism to assist the pioneer to practise the ministry that he or she is called to, or to release the potential of a fresh expression of church. They are generally a call for the ministry to be conducted in a manner that is familiar, and less demanding in some way. Interference can be subtle or blatant, but the end result is almost always the same. One pioneer minister had initiated a fresh expression of church for recovering drug addicts aged 30 and over. A highly influential church member who had worked with young drug addicts repeatedly interfered in the ministry by offering unwanted and ill-informed advice to both the church council and the pioneer minister. He was completely un-able to realize the extent of the difference between the problems of young teenage addicts and those of recovering older addicts. When he began turning up uninvited to meetings to give the group the 'benefit' of his advice and experience, membership of what had been a helpful and growing ministry declined rapidly.

Being unwilling to let go

Both churches and pioneers need to learn how to let go of a ministry when it takes on a natural Spirit-filled life of its own. Not letting go is like refusing to cut a child's umbilical cord and expecting a birthed child to continue to receive all its food and oxygen from the parent despite it having lungs and a stomach of its own. The need to enable and exit applies to churches as well as to pioneers. Not letting go of leadership, governance and power eventually kills both the fresh expression and the potential leadership it may have been nurturing.

There are many and several reasons for not wanting to let go, from the most positive, love of community, to the most negative, fear for the community. The online fresh expressions guide *Share* advises that pioneers and churches learn to cultivate a more 'Ascension day'-oriented theology. Jesus loved the community that he founded sufficiently to let go and entrust the ministry he had started into the care of those he had nurtured. It remained his ministry, but it was now a ministry which released the gifts and graces of others in a way that was not possible before.

Cole advises all pioneers to settle what he calls their 'ownership issues'. His advice is simple: pioneers and churches should stop being concerned about whether the ministry or fresh expression will succeed or not, it doesn't belong to them in the first place.

> Your reputation isn't on the line; Jesus' is. He will do a good job
> if we let him . . . It's time for faith that fears inaction not failure.[3]

Being too heavenly minded to be of any earthly use

The last cause of failure is in many ways the simplest to identify but the hardest to rectify. It happens when pioneers have grand ideas for the Church and a solution to the problem of decline. They know just how to enable the people to see the light, to respond to the gospel and to follow Christ. They have been given the vision of the New Jerusalem promised in the book of Revelation, and told just how to make it happen. They share their vision with others, with anyone who will listen, and work hard to cultivate support for their new ministry. They begin, as Jim Griffith notes, 'to believe everything they are saying and begin to consider as inevitable everything that they are dreaming'.[4] He calls it being 'drunk of their own vision', when pioneers become too heavenly minded to be of any earthly use. Too focused on what it is hoped God will do, to look down and see what God is already doing and has asked for the Church's help with. All successful ministry is rooted in service to God's people. It is when the Church is too busy looking heavenwards that it trips and stumbles most over the bodies of the poor and needy that Christ has brought to shelter in its rooms. Scripture makes it clear that there are no short-cuts to heaven, and while a vision of the Church of the future might well come true, it will undoubtedly only do so when the Church has learned how to carry all of God's people along with it.

Managing failure graciously

Fresh expressions of church and pioneer ministries are experimental, and it is in the nature of experiments to deliver results that are not what is expected. Thomas Edison's attitude provides the best response here. When talking of failed experiments he is reported to have said, 'I have not failed, I've just found 10,000 ways that won't work.'[5] A 'failed' fresh expression of church or ministry is simply a way of being church that hasn't worked at this time and place and in this particular way. It is not a sign of God's displeasure with the pioneer or the church, but may well be an aid to further discernment. The need to acknowledge the failure is, of itself, a gracious act. To fail to be honest about the possible causes of failure can only lead to greater misery later. The lack of opportunity to reflect critically on ministry can not only permanently damage the relationship between a church and a ministry; it can also inhibit any further exploration of pioneering ministry. The church needs therefore to be pastoral and loving enough to know that good closure is important to being able to move on in ministry and continue the work of God.

Managing failure graciously will therefore entail listening to the hurt and anger that closure sometimes generates and offering it back to God in prayer. The whole of the church needs to own the pain and the grief of the loss of something that has had considerable investment of time and energy given to it. The truth needs to be heard. 'Just because something doesn't do what you planned it to do doesn't mean it's useless.'[6] God invites the Church to take risks for the sake of the kingdom but makes no promises that the final outcome will be what the Church wants. God does what God wants, not what the Church wants God to do. Holding on to that is vitally important in this exciting, challenging time of growth and the renewal of adventure in mission and ministry.

One gracious way of managing the failure of a fresh expression or pioneer ministry is to hold a service or celebration of thanksgiving. This can be an opportunity to give thanks to God for the work of the Spirit and the opportunities that were provided for the community to grow in service and in the knowledge of God. The service should not be an attempt to put a gloss on an otherwise depressing event but rather a means of centring the whole of the ministry, including its ending, in the context of God's gracious will. The service could include an opportunity to hear the testimony of those who benefited from the fresh expression. Not only would this allow for the people concerned to share what God has given them, but it could also provide a means for the Spirit to speak about the work that might still need to be undertaken.

Former members of a fresh expression should be offered appropriate pastoral care and contact. This may mean creating and supporting a smaller 'cell' of those who are still interested in sharing in fellowship and ministry together, so that they have the space and the time to discern the will of God for their future. People's relationship with God is not a fad that can be taken up and put down again at a whim. The amount of love and care that a church shows to those who have been genuinely seeking to follow Christ is a true reflection of its own ability to seek and follow Christ.

The success of a pioneer ministry or fresh expression of church

What should a church do when a pioneering ministry transcends all expectations and a fresh expression of church grows to the point where it is larger than the inherited church that nurtured and supported it? Should it be concerned for its own continuity? How can it avoid either schism or division?

The answer to these questions is found in part in the knowledge that fresh expressions of church and pioneering ministry are not the invention of the Church; neither does the Church have a monopoly on them. God has never stopped working in the world, bringing people into community with Christ, finding ways to love the world and enable it to be reconciled through Spirit-filled ministry. The Church, however, is no longer strong enough to be able to ignore the pressure for change. It cannot depend on inherited membership, that is to say children becoming members as a result of their parents being members. It similarly cannot afford to ignore the consequent extent of church decline and still claim to be the representative of Christ here on earth. What signal does a declining Church send to the world about God?

For profoundly theological reasons as well as for obvious practical reasons, the Church must embrace the movement of the Spirit as it is discerned in each age. It must do so, however, without making a lie of all that it has been before. As Gabriel Fackre notes:

> The circle of tradition is not closed, for the Spirit's ecclesial work is not done. Traditional doctrine develops as Christ and the gospel are viewed in an ever fresh perspective. Old formulations are corrected, and what is passed on is enriched. The open-endedness however, does not overthrow the ancient landmarks. As tradition is a gift of the Spirit, its trajectory moves in the right direction although it has not arrived at its destination.[7]

Holding the tension between what the Church is and believes now, and what it has been and believed, is crucial to the success of all forms of fresh expression and pioneering ministry. The most successful or fruitful pioneer ministries are those which have been able to demonstrate their ability to initiate a form of church

> standing in solidarity with people in particular, given situations, while also not losing its universal, given identity – an identity which itself must remain particular and distinct in relation to other forms of society and global enterprise.[8]

A successful pioneering ministry or fresh expression in a mixed-economy church may therefore be a bridge between what is to come and what has already been and still is. There is no reason for it to be the cause or source of schism or division, but it can be a powerful catalyst for renewal and revision.

Change, renewal and revision

Churches are changed by successful fresh expressions. These changes might be physical, for example, as a result of trying to accommodate the needs of larger or different types of congregations. There could also be an apparent change in ethos or churchmanship as a result of different generations or cultures being thought of as members of the church. There will undoubtedly be financial changes either positive or negative, and ultimately there will be leadership and governance changes. Change that is not managed is usually destructive rather than creative, but change that is Spirit-led, embraced by the church and planned and prepared for, can sow a seed of renewal that might ensure continued growth for the next generation.

Managing success is about managing change, in the church as well as in business. Change usually involves three aspects: people, processes and culture. All too often the Church has placed the emphasis on the processes of being church – get the worship right or the structures right and everything else will follow. In fact, all three aspects are equally important if the change is to lead to further success. It is well known, for example, that most people are resistant to change, even change that they recognize as being necessary for their own future well-being. The history of the Church suggests that there are no easy solutions to overcoming this resistance. The Church can, however, learn and benefit from good business practices and begin to promote healthy change rather than try and force inevitable change. Not all change in the Church needs to be nailed to a door!

Good communication is essential – as is working with the prevailing culture even though it is the one that will ultimately be changed. Good communication means being prepared to be very clear about what is, and is not, being said. There is a reason why certain statements in the Bible are prefaced with 'says the Lord God of Hosts' or 'Truly truly I say to you'. In matters of faith where interpretation is often mistaken for factual truth, it is essential to distinguish between supposition and actuality, between what is important and what is desirable. But above all, good communication is about face-to-face conversation, Christian conferring at its best, so that the opportunities for misunderstandings are minimized. The incarnation happened so that the good news was more than hearsay. Promoting healthy change begins with open and honest communication within the prevailing culture about the gap between what is desirable and what is possible. Jesus worked from within Judaism to effect the change that sets us all free. He neither condemned it nor stood outside of it but used its systems and structures to try and communicate the necessity of change in dialogue with the priests and the scribes. Paul similarly used both his Jewish and his Roman identities to effect the changes in his life that were demanded by his Christian identity.

The spread of Christianity through the missionary endeavours of Paul and Barnabas demonstrates a further essential component of change, namely teamwork which is properly aligned to good leadership. Someone has to be willing to initiate change before it can begin, but the change itself should always be a shared responsibility. Paul introduced change into the Church by taking the requests of the Gentile converts to the council in Jerusalem. The Church that was emerging as a result of the pioneering ministry which he and others were practising was very much a 'fresh expression' of church to the rest of the Church at Jerusalem. Its customs were strange, its worship was different, its membership more culturally determined. Paul can only be credited with initiating these changes, however; the rest of the church leadership had to accept responsibility and play their part in making them happen.

Changes in the life of a mixed-economy church, such as possible modifications to the sanctuary or ancillary rooms, or even the availability or otherwise of certain resources, may seem petty in comparison to the big debates recorded in the Acts of the Apostles – but they too have their part to play in the revision and renewal of the Church. As was the case when the Gentile converts began to outnumber the Jewish converts in the early Church, certain changes or issues can become more pressing when a fresh expression matures such that those who attend it begin to outnumber those who attend the 'traditional' Sunday worship. Regardless of how they present, such issues are ultimately questions of power and authority, and are best dealt with by recognizing them as such.

Most churches have systems and structures in place which should ensure that power and authority are sensitively managed through good church governance. Part of the covenant relationship formed by setting the boundaries described earlier is an understanding that in the body of Christ, and hence in either the inherited or fresh expression of church, power can only be given and shared, not taken or held. Numerical weight alone cannot decide church polity or policy: in some churches, for example, there can be more tourists than worshippers visiting the premises, but there is no suggestion that the tourists should decide who the minister is, where the altar should be, or what the church should proclaim as its faith.

If a fresh expression of church matures to the point where it becomes capable of being self-funding, it will need to decide whether or not it wants to continue to be held within the body of the church. The overriding concern must always be, not for the 'success' or growth of the fresh expression, but for the nurture and care of all the people involved. The decisions taken at this time will be determined largely by the nature of the relationship between the leadership of the fresh expression and the leadership of the local church that has nurtured and supported it. If there is good communication between the fresh expression and the inherited church, then it is much easier to deal with any problems that 'success' may bring. The covenant that binds them can be renegotiated as part of a continued shared participation in the mission of God. This is infinitely preferable to an unholy squabble over who has the right to use a particular room or who should pay for the new pew Bibles!

The covenant determines the way in which the fresh expression of church is under the oversight of the church and how it works within its disciplines, whatever they might be. A decision to end a covenant (which may or may not entail leaving the wider denominational relationship) may mean that the fresh expression will need to develop its own forms of governance in accord with its core values and practices. This is not as easy as it might first seem. Even the most radical forms of polity can quickly begin to stifle ministry in a rapidly changing world context. It is usually preferable, even if it takes a little longer, to work to effect a positive change in the systems and structures that are believed to inhibit the growth of the fresh expression. The prevailing culture of church is best changed from within. Remaining in a covenant relationship, even if a move is made to new premises, allows for a continued sharing of resources, human and material, and testifies powerfully to the unity of the church.

One of the key questions that all successful fresh expressions eventually need to consider is how culturally determined their membership is. What will happen to the people who are currently associated with it when they are no longer part of that particular cultural scene? Is the young person who found Christ at a youth fresh expression simply expected to find another 'church' when he reaches 18 or gets married? What happens to the mum who has been attending Messy Church when her children no longer want to attend? What happens when the skateboard is replaced by a car, or the city scene is swapped for a suburban semi? Can the fresh expression continue to encourage growth in grace and holiness as its members mature and change throughout their life?

The answer is found in the fact that a 'successful' fresh expression is one that will have all the characteristics of 'church'. It will therefore be genuinely concerned for the ongoing pastoral care and continuing discipleship of its members. It is for this reason, above all, that the mixed-economy church is so important. Working within the inherited church, the leaders of a fresh expression can plan for and properly prepare for the pastoral transition of its membership if necessary. This ensures that it can remain focused on the particular vision that God has given to it without abandoning those it has been nurturing in the faith. This, of course, works both ways. If the fresh expression becomes so successful that it effectively does 'replace' the inherited church then it has a shared responsibility to provide for the pastoral care of the 'inherited' church members. It is not enough to simply say, 'they can go elsewhere'. In either case what is most often needed is another fresh expression of church. So the whole process of revision and renewal through the means of grace begins again.

Fresh expressions will inevitably give rise to new fresh expressions, and the resulting network can be a powerful expression of the unity and catholicity of the Church.

Evidence has shown repeatedly that pioneering ministry works best when it is allowed to work with the Church, rather than in spite of it. Fresh expressions are intrinsic to the Church; they grow from their commitment to a goal that is rooted in the Church and the life of Christian discipleship. The evident love of the Church as the body of Christ, which successful pioneering demonstrates, actually encourages others to transcend the frustrations, exacerbations and irritations about the Church's lack of cultural sensitivity that normally inhibit their participation.

The transformation of the Church by a successful fresh expression is a work of grace. All change is accompanied by grief, however. When things are changed, something is lost as well as gained, and not everyone will consider the gain worth the loss. Managing this pastorally is the real test of what it is to be church. Preaching resurrection and experiencing resurrection are very different. The empty tomb on Easter Sunday was preceded by a painful time of grieving, even by those who believed that they 'knew' what was to happen. The time for grief is an important part of the movement to new life and for the realization that nothing will ever be the same again. The Church is not only renewed by a successful fresh expression, it is revised. This is to be expected. There was clearly something different about the resurrected Christ, who was unrecognizable to even his closest friends and disciples. Until, that is, Christ performed the all-too-familiar works of grace: he broke bread, brought peace, equipped and empowered others to proclaim the coming of the kingdom. In this way too will the church that is renewed and revised by a fresh expression be able to be recognized.

Often, all that is really required to manage the changes provoked by a growing pioneering ministry or fresh expression of church, and so prevent schism, is for the inherited church to not snuff out the spark of love that the pioneer has for the church. The church doesn't have to agree with the style of ministry, or even attend the fresh expression of church (in fact most pioneers would rather regular members did not attend!). All that is asked is that the church tries to swallow its fears and give the ministry the chance to burn brightly, or to be extinguished according to how the Spirit fans the flames.[9] The church has to find the way to trust to the methods of oversight that it has put in place to safeguard the agreed boundaries and simply allow the ministry to grow and flourish. It does not matter if the fresh expression grows to be larger; the church is not in competition for souls, but is concerned to build up the body of Christ.

The growth of the kingdom, of more people learning to know and love Jesus, has been the Church's intent all along. This is what the Church prays for, plans for, waits for and works for. It makes no sense therefore for the Church to fear it – the kingdom is God's answer to the world's injustice and inhumanity, it is God's answer to the prayers of intercession made each week in church. We may not understand it, or even recognize it as church, but it is God's gift to each generation, and by God's grace we have been called to share in its making and to enjoy it.

> And this is my prayer, that your love may overflow more and more with knowledge and full insight to help you to determine what is best, so that on the day of Christ you may be pure and blameless, having produced the harvest of righteousness that comes through Jesus Christ for the glory and praise of God.   (Phil. 1.9–11)

Notes

Introduction

1 Donald E. Messer, *Reinventing the Church*, Religion Online, http://www.religion-online.org, 3 March 1998.

2 Alpha is a course that has been used by the Church for over 25 years and is designed to present the basic principles of the Christian faith to new Christians in a relaxed and informal setting. For more information see http://uk.alpha.org/

3 Timothy Keel, 'Love is of the Essence', in Jennifer Ashley (ed.), *The Relevant Church: A New Vision for Communities of Faith*, Lake Mary, FL: Relevant Books, 2004, pp. 67–77, as quoted by Jason Byassee, 'Emerging Model: A Visit to Jacob's Well', *The Christian Century*, 19 September 2006, pp. 20–4.

1 Defining

1 Steve Croft, *How Do Pioneers Learn?*, http://www.freshexpressions.org.uk/section.asp?id=2108, January 2009.

2 For more information please see http://www.acpi.org.uk/downloads/Ordained_Pioneer_Ministers_Guidelines.pdf

3 Steve Croft, *Exploring Pioneer Ministry: A short guide*, London: Church House Publishing, p. 3.

4 John Wesley, 'The Twelve Rules of a Helper' (1753), in *The Constitutional Practice and Discipline of the Methodist Church*, 17th edn, Peterborough: Methodist Publishing House, 1988.

5 Revd David Warnock, Methodist minister and Fresh Expressions practitioner in the Nene Valley Circuit of the British Methodist Church (personal communication).

6 See Fresh Expressions Phase II Prospectus, p. 3, http://www.sharetheguide.org/section1/1, June 2009.

7 John Shelby Spong, 'The Emerging Church: A New Form for a New Era', *The Christian Century*, 3–10 January 1979, p. 10.

8 Ronald Rolheiser, *Secularity and the Gospel*, New York: Crossroad, 2006, p. 47.

9 The Uniting Church in Australia, *Living and Believing within the Unity and Faith of the One Holy Catholic and Apostolic Church*, http://assembly.uca.org.au/doctrine/images/stories/resources/dwgliving believing.pdf, January 2009.

10 Extended Holy Communion is the practice of extending the hospitality of Christ's table and invitation to those who cannot attend a church service for reasons of ill-health or infirmity. A suitably trained person shares the bread and wine that have been taken from the main service with the person who could not attend, in a shorter, specially prepared service in the home or hospital.

11 These words are often used in the liturgy of the Church when the eucharistic bread is broken. See for example, *The Methodist Worship Book*, Methodist Publishing House, Peterborough: 1999, p. 194.

12 See http://www.freshexpressions.org.uk/section.asp?id=4443, April 2009.

13 For more information see http://www.freshexpressions.org.uk/section.asp?id=4273, April 2009.

14 Simon Hall as quoted in Eddie Gibbs and Ryan K. Bolger, *Emerging Churches*, London: SPCK, 2006, p. 273.

15 Gerard Kelly, *Retrofuture: Rediscovering our roots, recharting our routes*, Downers Grove, IL: Intervarsity Press, 1999, p. 212.

16 Rob Frost, David Wilkinson and Joanne Cox (eds), *The Call and the Commission: Equipping a new generation of leaders for a new world*, Milton Keynes: Paternoster Press, 2009.

17 Ian J. Mobsby, *Emerging and Fresh Expressions of Church: How are they authentically Church and Anglican?*, London: Moot Community Publishing, 2007, p. 52.

18 S. J. Grenz, 'Ecclesiology' in K. J. Vanhoozer (ed.), *The Cambridge Companion to Postmodern Theology*, Cambridge: Cambridge University Press, 2003, pp. 252–68.

19 Steve Croft, 'Talent Spotting', http://www.freshexpressions.org.uk/section.asp?id=3649, January 2009.

20 *Encouraging Lay Pioneer Ministry: Bishops' Guidelines for the development of lay ministry in fresh expressions of church*, 2009.

21 Connexional Fresh Expressions Scheme. Methodist Council Papers. 2007, section 5, http://www.methodistchurch.org.uk/downloads/coun_fe_031007_0777.doc

22 *The Works of John Wesley*, ed. T. Jackson, London, 1831, vol. 10, p. 485.

23 Croft, *How Do Pioneers Learn?*

24 Connexional Fresh Expressions scheme as published on http://www.methodist.org.uk/index.cfm?fuseaction=opentogod.content&cmid=1714, December 2008.

25 Reginald Bibby as quoted in Ronald Rolheiser, *Secularity and the Gospel*, New York: Crossroad, 2006, p. 47.

26 Charity Hamilton, Fresh Expressions practitioner in the Bristol District of the British Methodist Church (unpublished story of a pioneer minister).

2 Preparing

1 *Mission-Shaped Church*, London: Church House Publishing, 2004, p. 24.

2 Ray S. Anderson, 'A Theology for Ministry', in Anderson (ed.), *Theological Foundations for Ministry: Selected readings for a theology of the Church in ministry*, Edinburgh: T&T Clark, 1979, p. 7.

3 Charity Hamilton, Fresh Expressions practitioner in the Bristol District of the British Methodist Church (unpublished story of a pioneer minister).

4 Susan Smith, 'Gospel and Culture', *Missiology: An International Review* 34.3 (2006), pp. 337–48.

5 Bishops' Guidelines for Ordained Pioneer Ministers.

6 Roland Riem, 'Mission-Shaped Church: An Emerging Critique', *Ecclesiology* 3.1 (2006), pp. 125–39.

7 See http://www.messychurch.org.uk/

8 Neil Cole, *Organic Church: Growing faith where life happens*, San Francisco: Jossey-Bass, 2005, p. 177.

9 Cole, *Organic Church*, p. 175.

10 See http://www.churcharmy.org.uk/web/FILES/View_A_Edit_M/The _Bridge_-_Building_Bridges.pdf, April 2009.

11 Ray S. Anderson, *The Shape of Practical Theology: Empowering ministry with theological praxis*, Downers Grove, IL: InterVarsity Press, 2001, p. 56.

12 Michael Frost and Alan Hirsch, *The Shaping of Things to Come: Innovation and mission for the 21st-century church*, Peabody, MA: Hendrickson, 2003, p. 83.

13 Office for National Statistics, *Living Next Door: Social capital: support and involvement*, as published on http://www.statistics.gov.uk/ CCI/nugget.asp?ID=183, February 2009.

14 Ronald Rolheiser, *Secularity and the Gospel*, New York: Crossroad, 2006, p. 44.

15 Victoria Combe, in *Financial Times*, Arts & Weekend, 13 December 2008, also online at http://www.ft.com/cms/s/0/d8f3d2e2-c718-11dd-97a5-000077b07658.html?nclick_check=1

16 Frost and Hirsh, *The Shaping of Things to Come*, pp. 95–107.

17 Stanley Hauerwas and W. Willimon, 'Ministry as More than a Helping Profession', *The Christian Century*, 15 March 1989, pp. 282–4.

3 Pioneering

1 Steve Croft, *Meetings and Mission*: Acts 15 on http://www.fresh expressions.org.uk/section.asp?id=3680, January 2009.

2 Revd David Warnock, Methodist minister and Fresh Expressions practitioner in the Nene Valley Circuit of the British Methodist Church (personal communication).

3 Steve Croft, 'Talent Spotting', http://www.freshexpressions.org.uk/ section.asp?id=3649, January 2009.

4 Shena Woolridge, http://www.sharetheguide.org/comment1, 30 March 2008 – 13.24.

5 Lucie Clarkson, http://www.sharetheguide.org/comment1, 22 October 2007 – 23.17.

6 Start! is similar to Alpha but a much shorter basic six-session introduction to the Christian faith for use in small groups. For more information see http://www.start-cpas.org.uk/overview.htm

7 Ian and Erika Biscoe – Hayford Park on http://www.acpi.org.uk/ articles/Stories%20of%20Fresh%20Expressions%20of%20church.pdf

8 Duncan Petty, http://www.sharetheguide.org/comment1, 24 October 2007 – 11.15.

9 Susan Smith, 'Gospel and Culture', *Missiology: An International Review* 34.3 (2006), pp. 337–48.

10 Stanley Hauerwas and W. Willimon, 'Ministry as More than a Helping Profession', *The Christian Century*, 15 March 1989, pp. 282–4.

11 Neil Cole, *Organic Church: Growing faith where life happens*, San Francisco: Jossey-Bass, 2005, p. 175.

4 Maturing

1 See http://www.freshexpressions.org.uk/section.asp?id=3145&intpp= 1&txtValidateFXSearch=&s1=&s2=&s3=&s4=&s5=, February 2009.

2 Anglican Diocese of Norwich newsletter, *Outreach* 2.2 (May 2008).

3 Anglican Diocese of Newcastle newsletter, *Outreach* 2.2 (May 2008).

4 As found on http://www.freshexpressions.org.uk/section.asp?id= 2477&intpp=1&txtValidateFXSearch=&s1=&s2=&s3=&s4=&s5=, February 2009.

5 Article 19a of the Articles of Religion of 1563.

6 *Newsletter of the Church Army in Australia* 73 (March–April 2007).

7 Jason Byassee, 'Emerging Model: A Visit to Jacob's Well', *The Christian Century*, 19 September 2006, pp. 20–4.

8 Anne Maclaurin on *expressions the DVD*, 2: *changing church in every place*, 8: Sustaining fresh expressions.

9 Stuart Murray, *Church after Christendom*, Milton Keynes: Paternoster Press, 2004, p. 165.

10 Office for National Statistics, social trends.

11 Murray, *Church after Christendom*, p. 165.

12 Tim Keel, as quoted by Byassee, 'Emerging Model'.

13 Peter Steinfels, Obituary of John Howard Yoder, a Mennonite theologian, in the *New York Times*, 7 January 1998.

14 Steve Chandler, *100 Ways to Motivate Yourself: Change Your Life Forever*, 2nd edn, revised, Franklin Lakes, NJ: Career Press, 2004, p. 57.

15 Lyman Coleman, as quoted by Andy Sloan in *Pioneering the Small-Group Movement*, 9 August 2004, available online at http://www .forministry.com/vsItemDisplay.dsp&objectID=73724C17-CC2D-4DA2-BE45784740EEC212&method=display&templateID=C3435351-D45C-4B52-867A3F794D1CD85C, February 2009.

16 http://cole-slaw.blogspot.com/2008/12/youd-be-surprised-what-people-will-do.html

5 Mixed economy

1 Stanley Hauerwas and W. Willimon, 'Ministry as More than a Helping Profession', *The Christian Century*, 15 March 1989, pp. 282–4.

2 Rowan Williams, Archbishop of Canterbury, addressing the General Synod of the Church of England, July 2008.

3 Charity Hamilton, Fresh Expressions practitioner in the Bristol District of the British Methodist Church (unpublished story of The New Place).

4 John Patton, *Pastoral Care in Context: An Introduction to Pastoral Care*, Louisville, KY: Westminster John Knox Press, 1993, p. 39.

5 Roland Riem, 'Mission-Shaped Church: An Emerging Critique', *Ecclesiology* 3.1 (2006), pp. 125–39.

6 Statement by the Rt Revd Nigel McCulloch, Bishop of Wakefield as reported on http://www.cofe.anglican.org/news/statistics_can_be_a_tool_for_mission,_says_church.html, January 2009.

7 http://www.statistics.gov.uk/

8 Riem, 'Mission-Shaped Church'.

9 Ronald Rolheiser, *Secularity and the Gospel*, New York: Crossroad, 2006, p. 44.

6 Digging at the foundations

1 Neil Postman, quoted in Dan Kimball, *The Emerging Church: Vintage Christianity for new generations*, Grand Rapids: Zondervan, 2003, p. 133.

2 For more information see http://www.moot.uk.net/SitePage/ foundation.htm. Moot is considered by some to be a good example of a sacramental fresh expression of church.

3 See http://www.labyrinth.org.uk

4 Gareth Powell on *expressions the DVD*, 2: *changing church in every place.*

5 Premkumar Williams, 'Between City and Steeple', in Kevin J. Vanhoozer, Charles A. Anderson and Michael J. Sleasman (eds), *Everyday Theology: How to read cultural texts and interpret trends*, Grand Rapids: Baker Academic, 2007, p. 127.

6 Paul Ballard, 'The Church at the Centre of the City', *Expository Times* 16.8 (2005), pp. 253–8.

7 Ian Mobsby on *expressions the DVD*, 2: *changing church in every place.*

8 Stanley Hauerwas and W. Willimon, 'Ministry as More than a Helping Profession', *The Christian Century*, 15 March 1989, pp. 282–4.

9 Marcus Ramshaw on *expressions the DVD*, 2: *changing church in every place.*

10 See Luke 15.4–6.

11 N. Wolterstorff, *Art in Action*, Carlisle: Solway, 1997, p. 82.

12 Roland Riem, 'Mission-Shaped Church: An Emerging Critique', *Ecclesiology* 3.1 (2006), pp. 125–39.

13 http://www.cofe.anglican.org/info/yearreview/dec04/story1.html, January 2009.

14 Jeff Fisher, as quoted on http://www.calvin.edu/worship/stories/ architecture.php, December 2009.

15 Charity Hamilton, Fresh Expressions practitioner in the Bristol District of the British Methodist Church (unpublished story of The New Place).

7 Common boundaries

1 www.methodism.org.uk/downloads/co_883_210408.doc

2 *Church Times*, 27 June 2008.

3 Susan Hope, *Mission-Shaped Spirituality: The transforming power of mission*, London: Church House Publishing, 2006, p. 108.

4 Stuart Murray Williams, as quoted in Michael Moynagh, *emergingchurch.intro*, Oxford: Monarch Books, 2004, p. 113.

5 Roland Riem, 'Mission-Shaped Church: An Emerging Critique', *Ecclesiology* 3.1 (2006), pp. 125–39.

6 Riem, 'Mission-Shaped Church'.

8 Harvest

1 Dr John Sentamu, http://www.archbishopofyork.org/1229, 10 February 2009.
2 Neil Cole, *Organic Church: Growing faith where life happens*, San Francisco: Jossey-Bass, 2005, p. 203.
3 Cole, *Organic Church*, p. 206.
4 Jim Griffith and Don Nations, *Why Church Plants Fail*, http://www.gbod.org/umcncd.org/manual/whyplantsfail.html
5 *The World Book Encyclopedia*, London: World Book, 1993, vol. E, p. 78.
6 As quoted in Christine Finn, *Artifacts: An archaeologist's year in Silicon Valley*, Cambridge, MA: MIT Press, 2001, p. 90.
7 Gabriel Fackre, *The Christian Story, vol. 1: A Narrative Interpretation of Basic Christian Doctrine*, 3rd edn, Grand Rapids: Eerdmans, 1996, pp. 18–19.
8 Roland Riem, 'Mission-Shaped Church: An Emerging Critique', *Ecclesiology* 3.1 (2006), pp. 125–39.
9 I am indebted in this section to Keith Olbermann and his rhetorical insight on what is needed to allow something to flourish.

Further reading

Eddie Gibbs and Ryan K. Bolger, *Emerging Churches: Creating Christian community in postmodern cultures*, London: SPCK, 2006. A helpful book which explores emergent as well as fresh expressions of church. It includes a very informative section in which pioneers tell their stories in their own words.

Michael Frost and Alan Hirsch, *The Shaping of Things to Come: Innovation and mission for the 21st-century church*, Peabody, MA: Hendrickson, 2003. Although written from an Australian perspective, this book helps to make the connection between mission and pioneering, especially with regard to leadership and the skills needed by a pioneer and congregation to sustain growth.

*   *   *

Paul Ballard, *The Church at the Centre of the City*, Peterborough: Epworth Press, 2009.

Neil Cole, *Organic Church: Growing faith where life happens*, San Francisco: Jossey-Bass, 2005.

Mission-Shaped Church, London: Church House Publishing, 2004.

Michael Moynagh, *emergingchurch.intro*, Oxford: Monarch Books, 2004.

Stuart Murray, *Church after Christendom*, Milton Keynes: Paternoster Press, 2004.

Index